A CREDIBLE UTOPIA

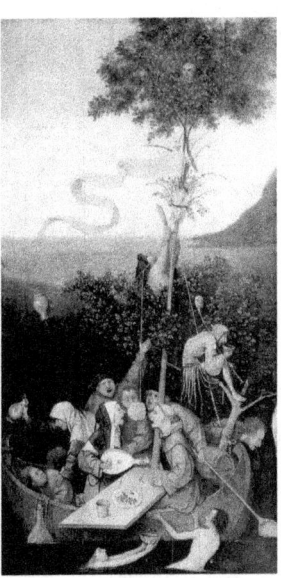

Fig. 1. Detail from Hieronymus Bosch, *Ship of Fools* (1490–1500)

First published in 2022 by punctum books, Earth, Milky Way.
https://punctumbooks.com

ISBN-13: 978-1-68571-056-9 (print)
ISBN-13: 978-1-68571-057-6 (ePDF)

DOI: 10.53288/0391.1.00

LCCN: 2022945025
Library of Congress Cataloging Data is available from the Library of Congress

Book design: Vincent W.J. van Gerven Oei
Cover image: Screenshot of Werner Schoeter, dir., *Der Tod der Maria Malibran* (1972)

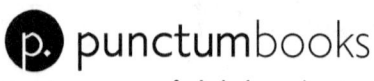

spontaneous acts of scholarly combustion

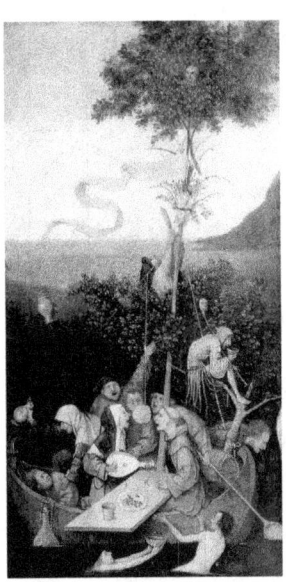

Fig. 1. Detail from Hieronymus Bosch, *Ship of Fools* (1490–1500)

First published in 2022 by punctum books, Earth, Milky Way.
https://punctumbooks.com

ISBN-13: 978-1-68571-056-9 (print)
ISBN-13: 978-1-68571-057-6 (ePDF)

DOI: 10.53288/0391.1.00

LCCN: 2022945025
Library of Congress Cataloging Data is available from the Library of Congress

Book design: Vincent W.J. van Gerven Oei
Cover image: Screenshot of Werner Schoeter, dir., *Der Tod der Maria Malibran* (1972)

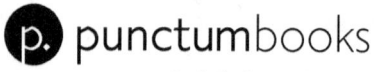

punctumbooks
spontaneous acts of scholarly combustion

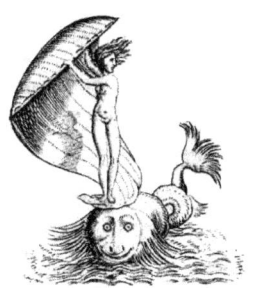

HIC SVNT MONSTRA

Peter Valente

A Credible Utopia
Essays on Selected Films of Werner Schroeter

p.

Contents

Acknowledgments

I'd like to thank Livy O. Snyder for her careful editing of the manuscript, and Vincent W.J. van Gerven Oei for all his hard work in its initial and final stages, as well as his interest in Schroeter's work. A special thanks to Eileen A. Fradenburg Joy for taking on the manuscript and seeing it though to print.

A Personal Journey over the Years
with the Films of Werner Schroeter

I remember attending the retrospective of Werner Schroeter's films in 2012 at the Museum of Modern Art in New York City. I attended most of the screenings because I had been aware of his name at the time, since I had watched many of the films from the so-called New German Cinema. I was immediately attracted to his films because they seemed so unusual compared to the other German films at the time. I admired the theatricality and almost unhinged emotional quality of the films. They seemed improvised and irreverent. Schroeter was a kind of romantic with both his feet in the real world. He writes in his autobiography:

> I hitchhiked from Heidelberg to Ludwigshafen to meet sailors in 1965 and 1966. How could it be anything but romantic to come close to others, and not only in one's thoughts and feelings? We wanted to experience real life…Back then there were gas lamps everywhere, and the BASF chemical factories blinked like something in a science fiction movie—a wonderful image of the night. There was a friendly tart, getting on in years, who wanted to adopt me. But instead I hitchhiked home at four in the morning and was driven to school by my mother. Love was an unknown feeling that I still wanted to

experience. To know love and then die — a death in love, a *Liebestod* — was an incredibly romantic notion.

They were films that did not take themselves too seriously even when dealing with serious subjects like the nature of love and death.

At the time of the retrospective in 2012, there was hardly anything in English[1] on his films and only one film available on DVD domestically, in America.[2] At the time, what seemed obvious eluded me. William E. Jones writes:

> Economics have played a role in Schroeter's invisibility, but political forces are at work as well. When film industries avoid gay subjects, especially in places where homosexual behavior is punishable by law, filmmakers wishing to get beyond the puritanical norm of simpering apologia or outraged exposés (or worst of all, silence) have few options: experimental filmmaking, pornography, or some combination of the two.

General audiences may be uncomfortable with the excessive quality of the films, the flamboyant aspect, the drag, the mannerisms, the queer performances, etc. which all reflect a gay sensibility. But perhaps there are other reasons that Schroeter's films are not better known. To fully appreciate a typical Schroeter film requires a certain familiarity with high European literature and art as well as opera and music in general. Ulrike Sieglohr writing about Deux, in his essay on Schroeter's *Deux,* "Divine Rapture," writes: "Although at the core extremely subjective, *Deux* also contains references to European art history

---

1   For a long time only Michelle Langford's *Allegorical Images: Tableau, Time, and Gesture in the Cinema of Werner Schroeter* (Bristol: Intellect Books, 2006) was the only book available in English. Recently, a collection of essays on his films was published, *Werner Schroeter* (Vienna: Österreichisches Filmmuseum; Synema-Gesellschaft für Film und Medien, 2018), edited by Roy Grundmann.

2   At the time, *Palermo or Wolfsburg* was the only available DVD from Facets.

and literature, and this balancing act, while doubtless intriguing for dedicated Schroeter followers, is likely too opaque for the uninitiated." His films are demanding in this respect and can be off-putting to some viewers. Schroeter relates a funny incident that happened at Cannes when his film *Deux* was shown there in 2002, which illustrates the way in Schroeter's films could be seen; he writes: "one critic wrote that he didn't understand it all, but he felt as if he had seen several centuries of European art history running past him. *Voilà*." I have mentioned Schroeter's name to professors who taught film at universities who, and if they had heard it, had, nevertheless, not seen any of his films.

Palermo or Wolfsburg was the first film I saw on DVD in 2011. It contrasted the excitement, enthusiasm, and passion that Schroeter saw as fundamental to the Southern Italian sensibility with the Northern German sensibility. But, as Paul B. Precido notes, in his book *An Apartment on Uranus,* the fictional reality of a North and South on a map is maintained for political reasons; this reasoning is less about geography and more about seeing the North as superior and the South as inferior:

> As the anti-colonialist critics Anibal Quijano, Silvia Rivera Cuscanqui, and Walter Mignolo teach us, the South does not exist. The South is a political fiction constructed by colonial prejudice. The South is an invention of modern colonial cartography: the combined effects of the trans-Atlantic slave trade and the growth of industrial capitalism, still in quest of new territories to use for the extraction of raw material.

We must collapse these vertical distinctions which enforce a duality of inferior and superior, and hack the power grid; imaginatively interrupt and redirect the flow of knowledge, moving through fissures and gaps, to arrive at a new language. Being born in the south of Italy, Schroeter's film helped me think about these distinctions.

During this time, I had also purchased a bootleg copy of *The Death of Maria Malibran.* Because of my passion for opera, I knew Maria Malibran was a famous opera singer who had never recorded and died from complications after falling from a horse; but, at the time, I knew nothing about the director, except for a brief reference to him in Katz's *Encyclopedia of Film* which was basically negative. As I watched the film over the years, I came to see Schroeter's obsession with death and its connection to love and the idea that self-realization is also linked with the death of the male: the desire of the transgender person to fully embody herself. For Schroeter, a Utopic space exists where love is not a problem and transgender men and women are free to express themselves. At the time, I wrote in my journal about *The Death of Maria Malibran*: "Each scene is composed mostly of the close-ups of two female faces (or in some scenes, transgender women, or sometimes three, with rarely a male face); in each scene, we see one face drawing closer to the other, in an attempt to kiss the other, overcome by unspeakable longing. As each brief scene comes to a close, the slow movement of the women stops. The figures are posed in a very stylized manner, and the effect of the lightning makes the faces almost appear unearthly, angelic, against a black background, with their lips barely touching, as in a painting by Giotto." I would eventually come to see many of Schroeter's films as they slowly made their way onto DVD.

I never found Schroeter's films perplexing or confusing as many others have. Watching his films is a kind of somatic experience. However radical his films appear on the surface, they all appeal to the eyes and to the body first. He is not a realist like Fassbinder, nor political in the same way. *Der Bomberpilot* flirts with Nazism, but it is ultimately not a political film like *The Marriage of Maria Braun*. He is more akin to a filmmaker like Méliès; he is a magician with the camera as Méliès was, able to evoke an entire world outside the real word, with its own laws, that defy gravity as we know it, and with its own sensibility. I think those who have experimented with making films can understand the films of Werner Schroeter intuitively.

I was first drawn to his films as a filmmaker; I've worked in 8mm, 16mm, and digital. When viewing his films, I asked myself questions like: how did he get that lighting to produce such an image? What kind of film did he use? What kind of camera? I also admired his use of texts from literature, such as the *Songs of Maldoror* by Lautréamont, which he used in two films: *The Death of Maria Malibran* and the late film, *Deux*. I admired the way he used music in his films to comment on a character's thoughts, or to conflict with what is on the screen. Most of my films did not contain dialogue but I made extensive use of different kinds of music, from opera, to popular music, to jazz. I imagine Schroeter must have been aware of Kenneth Anger's use of music in his films, the way it comments on the images and adds another dimension to what one is seeing on the screen. So, I approached Schroeter from the viewpoint of a filmmaker first, and not an academic.

After watching Schroeter's films over the years, I am continually astonished that he is not well known, and furthermore, why Criterion has not released any of his films to date. Growing up in the time when VHS tapes were all the rage, I was able to see so many films; it was as though everything came out on VHS tapes. In any case, with the advent of DVDs it was clear that the market controlled what would be released. Fassbinder can be coopted for political reasons, and his kind of Sirkian melodrama is generally appealing to a wider audience. Even gay films like *Fox and His Friends* are more about class than the homosexual lifestyle. Schroeter's films are more overtly gay in style and subject matter and as a result, if he's taught at all, it is in gender and queer studies programs. His films are sensual and erotic and exist in their own realm of fantasy and fascination. They are utopian in the sense that they exist in an idealized world of personal freedom. His aesthetic didn't change when he made more seemingly political films, it was always manneristic, stylized, and operatic, more than it was a statement of ideology. Fassbinder wrote the following about Schroeter:

> Werner Schroeter will one day have a place in the history of film that I would describe in literature as somewhere between Novalis, Lautréamont, and Louis-Ferdinand Céline; he was an 'underground' director for ten years, and they didn't

want to let him slip out of this role. Werner Schroeter's grand cinematic scheme of the world was confined, repressed, and at the same time ruthlessly exploited. His films were given the convenient label of 'underground', which transforms them in a flash into beautiful but exotic plants that bloomed so unusually and so far away that basically one couldn't be bothered with them, and therefore wasn't supposed to bother with them. And that's precisely as wrong as it is stupid. For Werner Schroeter's films are not far away; they're beautiful but not exotic. On the contrary.

Many filmmakers have also borrowed from Schroeter. Timothy Corrigan, in his essay, "Werner Schroeter's Operatic Cinema," writes about Schroeter's influence on German filmmakers:

Fassbinder 'definitely learned from Schroeter's films' and 'Daniel Schmidt is unthinkable without Schroeter.' Herzog has frequently admitted the importance of Schroeter to his development; and, according to Fassbinder, that recent de-miurge of German filmmaking in America Hans-Jurgen Syberberg is little more than a 'merchant of plagiarism,' 'an extremely capable Schroeter imitator, who while Schroeter helplessly awaited recognition competently marketed what he took from Schroeter.

Fassbinder called Schroeter the white angel, whereas he saw him-self as the black angel: Fassbinder was sexually sadomasochistic and Schroeter was femme. He loved women for their femininity, for the way they moved, sang, or gestured. On the screen, his women are sensual. Schroeter's women were not the kind of di-rect political tool they were for Fassbinder. Schroeter may have been a feminist but he didn't have to be one; Magdalena Mon-tezuma was his muse and appeared in many of his films before she succumbed, years before he did, to the cancer that would eventually kill him. Isabelle Huppert was Schroeter's muse in his final years. She appeared in his next to last film, *Deux*; in that film, Schroeter capitalized on her fame. In some sequences the lighting is so brilliant that her face radiates a youthful determination and inner confidence, while also being tender and occasionally, unsure of herself. Her range of emotions in this film is brilliant. Schroeter would write about her: "Isabelle Huppert and I have been great friends ever since Malina. Even after work on that film was over, we remained close and regarded our friendship as a great gift. Isabelle is very intuitive and has a calm center, a harmonious strength, that she has worked to find for herself, making it her own by dint of experience." As the credits roll at the end of *Deux,* Huppert appears radiant, a white angel, indeed; it is a truly memorable scene.

Schroeter was more of an idealist than a strictly political filmmaker. In each of these films, his yearning for a Utopia can be seen. They call on the viewer to examine their own life and to consider their right to express themselves, even in an oppressive society. The final sentence in Schroeter's autobiography seems to encapsulate why his films are so important and why I consider them essential viewing. Schroeter speaks of our "overwhelming longing" for "a credible Utopia," despite our "full awareness of disaster, despite torture, viciousness, and intrigues." This "hopeful hopelessness and hopeless hope" is the central theme in the films of Werner Schroeter.

Works Cited

Corrigan, Timothy. "Werner Schroeter's Operatic Cinema." *Discourse* 3 (1981): 46–59. https://www.jstor.org/stable/41371588.

Fassbinder, Rainer Werner. "Chin-up, Handstand, Salto Mortale—Firm Footing: On the Film Director Werner Schroeter, Who Achieved What Few Achieve, with *Kingdom of Naples.*" In *The Anarchy of the Imagination: Interviews, Essays, Notes,* edited by Michael Töteberg and Leo A. Lensing, translated by Krishna Winston, 17–53. Baltimore: Johns Hopkins University Press, 1992.

Grundmann, Roy, ed. *Werner Schroeter.* Vienna: Österreichisches Filmmuseum; Synema-Gesellschaft für Film und Medien, 2018.

Jones, William E. *But Our Life Depends on What's Real.* Los Angeles: Semiotext(e), 2014.

Preciado, Paul. *An Apartment on Uranus.* Los Angeles: Semiotext(e), 2019.

Schroeter, Werner, and Claudia Lenssen. *Days of Twilight, Nights of Frenzy.* Translated by Anthea Bell. Chicago: University of Chicago Press, 2017.

THE SIXTIES

Schroeter's Experimental Films

Repression and Freedom: On Werner Schroeter's *Neurasia* (1968)

Werner Schroeter's early experimental film, *Neurasia,* contains the purist expression of his romantic and dramatic sensibility. With minimal props and a bare setting, four characters act out a drama that includes pain, pleasure, the glory of self-expression, and the violence of repression, accompanied by a soundtrack including Ethel Waters, Ruth Etting, Sophie Tucker, Aunt Jemima, and Percy Sledge. When a character is offered the possibility of a heterosexual relationship, it always ends in pain and confusion. But the one who asserts their independence from this coupling will dance and sing and express their individual selves. This film is Schroeter's fierce assertion of his independence as a filmmaker, and even here, he foreshadows his late film, *Deux,* with the problem of the double, the couple, as it relates to the realization of one's identity.

As the film opens, we see four people, three women (actresses Carla Aulaulu, Magalena Montezume, and Rita Bauer) and one man (actor Steven Adamczewski). Schroeter writes about these early friendships:

I had made good friends during that year [1968] of working in 8mm. I was thinking of those friends, Magdalena, Carla, and the others, and of a kaleidoscopic pattern, a selection from themes close to my heart that were developing in my mind like a wide horizon. The idea was to present our sense of life, the demands we made on ourselves, and achieve a change in our usual habits and the way we saw things. The group was an aesthetic movement, an aesthetic revolution, running parallel to the political events of 1968. I received compliments on that at the time, and I still do. My work was seen as the breaking of windowpanes that had become dull...I didn't want anything to do with psychological cinema, preferring the free interplay of music and film. But of course I also encountered a great deal of hostility.

In the opening scene, Rita is on her hands and knees, at the center of the screen; Carla is above her, standing on a couch, but the overall effect appears as if Carla is standing on top of Rita. Magdalena stands to the far right of the screen, and Adamczewski is to the far left of the screen. Thus, a power dynamic is set up early in the film. The central struggle will be between Carla and Magdalena, between freedom and domination; the man will be inconsequential in the beginning of the film. Magdalena gives the man across from her a quizzical look as if to say that she is jealous of Carla's show of independence. There is no sound at this point. Magdalena says something to Carla; but she responds by laughing and taking a sip of her wine. Magdalena and Adamczewski are in awe of her. At one point, early in the film, he hands Magdalena a kind of demonic talisman. Later, he and Magdalena are seen worshipping and offering up prayers to the talisman. Carla wants no part this cult of worship, which we will discover is a force for repression, and would rather drink, dance, and freely express herself.

Carla, seeing a naked man (Admczewski) crawling across the floor, moves towards him, and grieves over his apparent, dead body. The male must die for her to fully realize herself. For Schroeter, this is an idea he will explore more fully in *The Death of Maria Malibran*: the male must die in order for the trans woman to emerge. In the next scene, she begins her triumphant dance sequence, which will continue throughout the film, fanning herself. In one scene, the man from Magdalena's cult approaches Carla, gets down on one knee, and affectionately places his head on her belly. He represents a figure of death to Carla, because he is sexually repressed. Throughout the film, Adamczewski either accompanies Carla on the guitar, or is Magdalena's slave. The heterosexual male figure of strength and aggression, an ideal in Nazi Germany, is here passive, unsure of himself, gay, and repressed.

As Carla continues to dance in a flamboyant manner, Magdalena and Rita look on with boredom and indifference. At one point, they try to force Carla onto her knees, to stop her from expressing herself, while we hear on the soundtrack, the voice of Ethel Water's singing her song "Am I blue," with the lines, "I'm just a woman, I'm only a woman, waiting on the weary shore, I'm just a woman, only human." When Magdalena is alone with the man, he appears indifferent to her, and is in his own world. Ethel Waters continues to sing about love lost while Magdalena is in agony, presumably because of the man. Schroeter cuts the song prematurely at the line, "Was I gay," allowing it to resonance with a meaning it didn't have in Ethel's time. Then there is a cut to the man's face. Through cutting Schroeter reinforces the idea in the film that the man is gay. He continues to court Magdalena but to no avail. He remains her puppet and submissive to her. Even in this early film, Schroeter seems to be critical of gay men attempting to find a relationship with straight women, thus ignoring their true identity. But he was never militant like his friend, Rosa von Pranheim.

While Magdalena continues to suffer in her relationship with the gay man, Carla flirts with one of the women in the cult since she identifies primarily with women rather than men. In identifying with women, Carla/Schroeter was trying to realize her identity. While Magdalena and Adamczewski seem in a trance, robotic, as they drift, listlessly across the screen, Carla is seen dancing and enjoying herself; she is alive, awkward, charming, an amateurish dancer, but fully confident, and comfortable with herself.

Magdalena marries the repressed man. In one scene, his hands are folded in prayer, while she is wracked by pain. She finds release in offering her life to the demonic talisman, while he is praying, perhaps to be cured of what he sees as a *sexual disease*. He goes to Carla for comfort. Carla plays a singer in this film as she would do again in *Der Bomberpilot*. Here we see her performing, in an elegant black dress, for an audience. As Magdalena and the man continue to worship the idol, Carla tests the limits of her sexual identity, by dressing in leather, in elegant dresses, and in drag, experiencing both pain and pleasure, and flamboyantly femme.

Even as Magdalena is trying to assuage the pain of her friend, Rita, presumably also suffering from a failed relationship, we see Carla singing, with one hand on her hip and another on her leg, a posture that asserts her feeling of independence, as if to say that she will have no part in the pain of coupling. In this film, Magdalena also appears in her guise as a lesbian cult leader who asserts her domination over two people, as she would, later on, in *Willow Springs,* though here she dominates a man and a woman. At one point, Carla is seen approaching the camera, holding the hand of Adamczewski, who is on her left, and Magdalena, on her right. Carla appears to be in a trance as a result of being in their grasp; it is a result of their brainwashing her. But she breaks free of the spell when she lets go of their hands and is alone. Then she begins to move her body slowly, improvising various dance steps; this is a private dance, for no one else, and just an expression of herself; it is as though she is in dialogue with herself, as she moves, or rather slowly undulates; she is casual, awkward, sensual, free.

Carla Aulaulu is wonderful in the film; she is possessed of a childlike ability to radiate internal emotions with a controlled intensity. She is not afraid to look directly at the camera, demanding to be seen and heard on her own terms. The accompaniment of the Hawaiian music on the soundtrack, and her subtly masculine features, gives the feeling of a drag performance. Roy Grundmann writes, in "The Passions of Werner Schroeter":

> Schroeter's cinema of stylized if deliberately amateurish or imperfect gestures and fleeting allusions to popular culture has a long tradition in queer circles — for instance, in the experimental wing of the downtown New York dance scene... but also in the mundane acts of queer fandom as practiced, for instance, by gay men re-enacting their favorite movie scenes. The way Adamczewski and Montezuma handle Aulaulu as he collapses in performed hysteria is reminiscent of feverish Hollywood melodramas that queer audiences reperform in a utopian spirit, refusing to separate victimization and suffering from resistance and survival.

And the effect of Carla continuing to dance in this awkward manner and unafraid to express her femininity, as Percy Sledge sings, "I'm sending a prayer up to heaven for you return" creates the oddly sensual effect of her overall performance. She is a young boy, a young girl, a woman, a man; in her dancing, she inhabits, even for a brief moment, different genders as a result of her physique and the way Schroeter films her.

Magdalena and the man continue be part of a cult of repression, symbolized by the magic talisman; Magdalena is seen gazing in a trance at the talisman on the wall. Eventually, both she and the man surround Carla and interrupt her dancing; they pick her up and lay her on the ground. She eventually dies. Repression wins over free expression. This is story of '68 again: revolutionary action unable to change the basic foundation of oppression.

In his autobiography, Schroeter writes about the reception of the film:

> Someone from a Bavarian film club for young people called *Neurasia* a 'Schroeter musical'; in Munich such films were shown in the Other Cinema. That was roughly the kind of reaction we wanted. The film critic Fieda Grafe called *Neur-*

asia a 'stage for language.' In the magazine Filmkritik, which was very important to me, she wrote: '*Neurasia* is a silent film with music. The tunes fit with the images as they used to in the days when the pianist was still sitting in the auditorium. Sometimes you have the illusion of synchronicity, until the music breaks off and Carla opens her mouth wider. You can see that she is sometimes singing silently, sometimes speaking silently. You can understand her. In the elevated sphere in which the film moves there are no such concepts as idol, adoration, star, myth, ecstasy. Nothing exists but the ultimate sense, the highest meaning.' She also linked my film to Witold Gombrowicz's illuminating comment on "the divine silliness of operetta," which pleased me tremendously.

On the surface, *Neurasia* is a film that could be described as an operetta, but in fact, is a dark film about repression and the attempts of society, embodied by Magdalena, Adamczewski, and Rita, who worship the demonic talisman, to crush any signs of freedom and joy, embodied here by Carla's pagan lifestyle. Society stands for law and order, the individual for freedom and independence. One is always in conflict with the other. The situation of a trans man or women in a heteronormative society is precarious and often dangerous. Femme men are particularly at risk. The early scene in *Deux*, where a sailor beats up a gay man who is cruising in a park at night, is a reminder that, even in 2002 (the release of the film), with the war for gay rights apparently won, gay men are never safe in a society where all mainstream images depict heterosexual men and woman coupling. This is one of Werner Schroeter's most important early films, where all his mannerisms, theatricality, and love for music, are on full display.

Works Cited

Grundmann, Roy. "The Passions of Werner Schroeter." In *Werner Schroeter,* ed. Roy Grundmann, 2–56. Vienna:

Österreichisches Filmmuseum; Synema-Gesellschaft für Film und Medien, 2018.

Schroeter, Werner, and Claudia Lenssen. *Days of Twilight, Nights of Frenzy.* Translated by Anthea Bell. Chicago: University of Chicago Press, 2017.

2

Ideality and Violence: On Werner Schroeter's *Aggression* (1968)

Werner Schroeter's 22 min. film, *Aggression,* shot in black and white on 16mm, opens with a close up of a woman's face (Heidi Lorenzo) holding a rose up to her lips, gently kissing it, and moving it across her cheek, as if immersing herself in its scent. The rose, of course, has a long and elaborate history, in literature and art, of representing the ideal in love and beauty; in Christian iconography it symbolizes heaven and the Virgin Mary. It is red, because Aphrodite wounded herself and stained the flower with her blood. The rose also has a long history in Iran and other surrounding regions; in the ghazel, the rose is associated with the sound of the nightingale, with its sound of longing. In the first image of the film, we see the young woman, who longs for the ideal of love. Instead, she is met with the aggressive force of a man she meets in the park. The man also appears in stairwells, entrances to bathroom, and turnstiles. The threat of violence is impersonal and everywhere in a male dominated world. In fact, in keeping with the mysterious nature of the man in the film, for many years the identity of the actor was not known. Over the years it been suggested that actor's name was Knut Koch and this was later proven to be true.

The film is silent except for a voiceover, which may or may not be the woman. These texts speak of bucolic surroundings, the need for Christian values, and the destruction of immoral, depraved behaviors. Grundmann writes, that "this was conservative middle class culture's response to the sexual revolution and the advent of Women's Lib…other statements consist of petit-bourgeois platitudes against the counterculture." If we read these words as the woman's own, then it is as if she has internalized this ideology and become the victim. But if we read this as just the ideal of a conservative ideology spoken by someone other than the woman, then it is the man who has not respected a woman's right to freedom and the film becomes a feminist critique of male *Aggression*. And I think this also extends to the treatment of gay and trans men and woman. The women in Schroeter's films often contain masculine features. Lorenzo has broad shoulders, a wide jaw, and is not conventionally feminine; her face seems to slip between genders as a result of the quick movements of her face and body.

The man is an aggressor both at the first meeting and later when he and the woman are having sex. The woman misreads the signals of his *Aggression* and lets him go to bed with her. Or perhaps she is raped. In either case, the sex is not pleasing to her nor to him, or rather his *Aggression* in bed may be the result of his *conscious* attempt to show that he virile. There is no tenderness or love. The man is dangerous and will kill her out of his own insecurity about his sexual identity. This film is also a critique of heterosexuality, and the coupling of a man and woman. However, the difference between this film and *Neruasia* or *Argila,* and their similar treatment of the subject, is that here the outward aggressive nature of straight coupling and sex is obvious, rather than repressed.

In her book *Reverse Cowgirl,* McKenzie Wark writes,

As everybody supposedly knows, us faggots are even less than women. Plenty of straight women would agree, and, sad to say, so too would some lesbians. The non-straight world was not free of its obsessive ranking and sorting. It was not communism. I wanted to destroy all of this.

The femme male is at risk. My claim here is that Lorenzo is both the woman in the film, and, in another respect, the femme male; in either case, heterosexuality is at fault in perpetuating these hierarchies that are aggressively maintained by the male. As Roy Grundmann writes: "It bears noting that many of the qualities Kuhlbrodt identifies in Schroeter's early work are classic characteristics of Queer Cinema…his gender non-conforming performers embody and enact transgressive desires." This is clear in the later films of the early period, in the late 60s and early 70s, but if one sees the physical characteristics of the woman contains masculine aspects, and that she is essentially "virgin" as symbolized by the rose, she can be read as a gay man who transitioned to a trans woman. On the surface we have a heterosexual coupling that is based on *Aggression,* but Shcroeter's choice of actresses and his filmmaking style also give the film this second layer of meaning.

In both *Argila* and *Aggression,* the man dies at the conclusion of the film. In *Aggression,* we can see the victim enacting violence against the abuser. But as Magdalena, in *Argila,* casually walked away after she sees that Hans is dead, Lorenzo appears, at the far right of the screen, looking at something in front of her, but we do not know at first what she is looking at. She seems curious, as if she doesn't recognize what is before her. As the camera slowly pans to the right, the dead body of the man appears, laying over a mound of earth; the positioning of the body and this slow reveal eroticizes it. The body is erotic in death. But we did not actually see her kill him. So we don't exactly know how he died except that she might have had something to do with it. Nevertheless, his death was necessary for the inner logic of the film to complete itself, whether or not she killed him. The transition from the male to the female gender is complete; the film is now in drag.

Works Cited

Grundmann, Roy. "The Passions of Werner Schroeter." In
Werner Schroeter, ed. Roy Grundmann, 2–56. Vienna:
Österreichisches Filmmuseum; Synema-Gesellschaft für
Film und Medien, 2018.

Wark, McKenzie. *Reverse Cowgirl.* Los Angeles: Semiotext(e),
2020.

3

Checking Out of Hotel Loneliness: On Werner Schroeter's *Argila* (1969)

Werner Schroeter's short film, *Argila,* opens in black and white with Carla Aulaulu, on the left side of the screen, moving her mouth, and gesticulating, but there is no sound. After about 30 seconds, another image of her appears on the right side of a double screen projection, in color, and we realize that this is an image of her lip-syncing to a version of the Leon Carr and Earl Shuman classic "Hotel Happiness," made famous by Brook Benton, with the lyrics, "I'm checking out of the Hotel Loneliness…I'm checking into Hotel Loveliness since I found you… gonna make my new address Hotel Happiness." As she lip-syncs, on the right side, to a recording of the song by an unidentified woman, her voice sometimes synchronizes with the lyrics and other times it doesn't. On the left side, she is moving her mouth and it is totally out of sync with the recording to such an extent that it seems she is talking rather than singing. The soundtrack appears distinct from the two images, a kind of space that seems more immediate. Thus the female voice on the soundtrack is as if disembodied with little or no relation to the images.

Carla, in both images, moves in an awkward and yet queerly personal way, and that along with the soundtrack actually contains a certain charm. This is a unique quality of Schroeter's early films: the private is made public. She is unabashedly sensual, and unashamed of her sexuality. The camera is her mirror, and she sees only herself, exulting in her performance, hamming it up, so to speak, and there is no attempt to be graceful, appropriate, or poised; she is sexually free, obeying no law but her own desire. Altogether, it is part of an amateur performance, but it is, nevertheless, an assertion of freedom, albeit one only possible in this alternate space that the film creates.

This is a unique quality of Schroeter's early films; the private is made public. Carla is unabashedly sensual, and unashamed of her sexuality. The camera is her mirror, and she sees only herself, exulting in her performance, hamming it up, so to speak, and there is no attempt to be graceful, appropriate, or poised; she is sexually free, obeying no law but her own desire.

After a few seconds, a man[1] and a woman (Magdalena) appear, on the left side of the double screen projection, in black and white, on the corner of a street. They are facing each other. The private space of unregulated behavior gives over to the harsh sounds of the street, with an imposing building in the background; the two people seem dwarfed by the size of the large building. The effect is like waking from a lovely dream with the sound of a loud alarm clock. On the right side of the screen, in color, we see the man and woman walking along a street. On the left side, they have arrived at a destination. Effect precedes cause and the present contains the memory of the past. Magdalena says to him, "I worship you and you don't care." On the left side, the scene, in black and white again, changes to reveal an older woman, who begins reading from a letter. Soon after a delay of 30 seconds, the right side of the screen, in color, shows the same woman reading a letter to Magdalena. In the letter, written presumably to the man, whose name we now know is Hans, Magdalena writes: "you embody death for me. It is my destiny," echoing the situation in *Neurasia,* where the repressed gay man will appear as an image of death. It also suggests the Nazi ideal of death before dishonor, the cult of death so embedded in Nazi ideology. In the next scene, Magdalena

---

1   This man remains anonymous until his identity is later revealed.

gazes at his sleeping body as if searching for any possible sign of emotion from him, even as he sleeps, any sign of life. She also admires his physique, which causes her despair, because he is not sexually available.

Growing desperate, at the dinner table, she says to him, "You want me to die. You have no pity for me.... I worshipped you. Tell me what I must do." Throughout her protestations, he remains silent. The older woman tries to show some affection for the man by kissing him softly and stroking his hair, but he remains asleep on the bed, and unresponsive at the beginning of the film but this will change as the film progresses.

Meanwhile, Magdalena realizes she doesn't and cannot understand him. The man is a cipher, a closed book, that will not open for her. She wanders through empty rooms alone; what appears to be a mirror is, in fact, a ring around a blank wall. In one scene, Magdalena unbuttons his shirt on the bed, but he is unmoving; he remains a living corpse to her. She demands a response from him, but he just stands before her with his arms folded across his chest. In one scene, he is walking down the stairs, apparently ready to go out, but she is at the bottom of the stairs waiting for him, to stop him from leaving. We learn that he opens up when he with the older woman; he is on his knees before her, and like a baby he leans his head against her belly. He reminds her of her child who had died. But he continues to remain emotionally unresponsive to Magdalena, who, perhaps in a fit of jealousy, keeps repeating to him "You want me to die. You take no pity on me." Earlier in the film, she accused the older woman of sleeping with him.

The older woman says, and repeats the words throughout the film, like an ominous mantra, that "Before the night is over, some misfortune will hurl us into a sea of desperation." We discover that the older woman is Magdalena's mother. She tells Magdalena that she must obey her out of duty. Here, Schroeter is showing an affinity with the genre of melodrama, by depicting the typical rivalry between mother-daughter for the affections of a handsome man, who happens to be the daughter's boyfriend. The man is friendly to the older woman; they talk and laugh while Magdalena, seated next to them, just stares into space, looking away. Hans feels that he can open up to the older woman because there is no threat of sexual desire. He is a narcissus, a beautiful man, so in love with himself, that he cannot love a woman. He is Orpheus, rejecting Euridice. He is, finally, a figure of death to Magdalena. Gay men will often build relationships with older, straight, women, because they identify with them, emotionally, but not sexually.

Near the end of the film, Madgalena is seen embracing the man, on the train tracks, as if this was the last time they would see each other; but the forced expression of emotion on his part, leads to his death. The man falls down on the tracks, lifeless. Soon after, the older woman appears, and puts her arms around his dead body, in a moment of despair. Magdalena casually picks up her purse and walks away. She seems indifferent to his death. In one sense, she has killed him by forcing him to simulate an emotion he does not have towards her. But, more importantly, he has killed himself by repressing his actual feelings (as a gay man). Silence = death.

Carla then appears on the left side of the screen, singing, and then on the right, in color, stilling singing without any sound. The figure of freedom still lives on. I would maintain, that on an allegorical level, Carla is the trans version of the man. Unable to maintain a gay lifestyle, the femme man is more comfortable being trans. More generally, Carla's exuberant, unashamed, display of her body, dancing and gesticulating, gives her performance the quality of drag. In *Neurasia,* Carla, a figure of independence and freedom, is crushed by the forces of authority. In *Argila,* she is reborn, as the man dies, to continue singing her song of freedom and hope, amplifying, as she does, her femininity and sexuality. These films are companion pieces and should be watched back-to-back since they are like two sides of a record, one a song of despair and the other a song of joy.

In his essay, "The Passions of Werner Schroeter," Roy Grundmann speaks about why Schroeter chose to film Argila in a double-screen projection:

According to his biography, the reason Schroeter conceived *Argila* as a double-screen film was to give spatial expression to the relationship triangle between a young man (Sigurd Salto), a woman his age (Magdalena Montezuma), and an older woman (Gisela Trowe). Their various on-screen constellations are doubled by the projection, whereby the image projected on the left side is re-projected on the right in flipped form and with approximately 30 second delay....A time delay between both projections creates an undulating visual tension between both sides.

On the left side is the effect and on the right side is the cause of an action. In "fusing two temporal levels into one, Schroeter effectively identifies cinema's presentness to always carry its own past." But "while the image comprises the temporal dimension of present and past, the sound, according to Schroeter, adds a third one — that of the future — whereby, as he states in his comments on film, all three levels are fused into the dimension of the eternal." Schroeter does not explain how his use of sound can achieve this effect. But music, unlike an image, is non-referential; sound may accompany an image but essentially exists apart from that image: we saw, earlier in the film, two images of Carla moving their lips to the lyrics of a song where there was an asynchronicity between the images and the soundtrack. In this way, Schroeter creates two temporal dimensions, simultaneously past and present, with the soundtrack acting as a third one; The disorientation this creates in the viewer suggests a kind of alternate space in the film, composed of the two images and their relation to the soundtrack, that is hard to describe. Perhaps this is what Schroeter meant by the eternal: a space that is felt more than it can be explained, an ideal space of infinite possibility. Carla only appears at the beginning and at the end of the film, and is not part of the drama of the film. While she is also subject to time, as the others are, she also represents an angel of the film outside of time. In any case, she is, as the song says, checking into a new address, the Hotel of Happiness, so the film ends on a provisional note of hope. But this ideal space in the film cannot last in reality. Odds are, she'll eventually have to check out of the hotel and deal with the harsh realities of the real world.

Works Cited

Grundmann, Roy. "The Passions of Werner Schroeter." In *Werner Schroeter,* ed. Roy Grundmann, 2–56. Vienna: Österreichisches Filmmuseum; Synema-Gesellschaft für Film und Medien, 2018.

4

"Life Is Very Precious, Even Right Now": On Werner Schroeter's *Eika Katappa* (1969)

Werner Schroeter's *Eika Katappa,* shot in color on 35mm film and clocking in at two hours and 22 minutes, is the culmination of the period of filmmaking that began in 1968 with *Aggression.* In a very short time, Schroeter developed radical ideas about filmic time, his manneristic style, theatricality, and experimental use of sound and image. The trajectory of this film is from a mythical space, where dramatic scenes from Verdi and Puccini's operas are re-enacted in the stylized manner that we've come to recognize as Schroeter's trademark, to an industrial, modern space, of factories, excessive traffic, and random noises. The sublime sounds of Callas's voice, and the drama of opera, give way to the mundane and harsh sound of car horns, and a landscape of industrial buildings; the movement is from this sublime space, to the domestic space of a home in Naples, where time is precious. In this harsh domestic space a father expresses his anger at his gay son, fearing for his safety when he goes away with a young man he met. But what links all these various scenes, whether in an operatic space or a domestic, is desire and love and their culmination in death.

Eika Katappa, opens, significantly, with Maria Callas singing the "Sempre Libera" aria from Verdi's *La Traviata.* Violetta is intoxicated and singing of her desire not to be bound to any lover, but to be able to move from one to another in her pursuit of various pleasures. She can hear Alfredo in the distance, singing that "love is the pulse of the universe." Thoughts of this love he has for her, causes Violetta to become pensive; but she quickly resumes her singing about how personal freedom is more important than being in love, which she sees as a limitation on her unbounded desire for pleasure. As we hear Callas singing on the soundtrack, we see Gisel Trowe, the actress playing Violetta, miming the words. Sometimes it seems as though the movements of her mouth synchronize with the words of the opera, but more often, it seems that the words don't synchronize; yet the point of the scene is how she moves her body. She throws up her arms, as if overcome with thoughts of liberation conveying the emotion of the aria and the music, its theme of sexual freedom, rather than there being a perfect one to one synchronization between the music on the soundtrack and the image. This is a familiar use of sound and image in Schroeter's films in order to show that perfection stands for the law and regulated behavior, while unrestricted freedom can take on many forms and many gestures, however amateurish, primitive, and even childish.

In one sense, it seems as though she is listening to a recording, and dancing as we do when we are alone and listening to music. In this way, it is a very private and intimate moment, but one that resonates with a wider more dramatic space, as if her experience of the music heightens her sense of freedom and extends her perception of possibilities, which are, nevertheless, also complicated by the desire to feel loved and to experience love. After the conclusion of the scene, we see an image on the screen, which will reappear throughout the film: it is of two hands, holding a rose, upright, with a chain binding the wrists together. We encountered the prominence of the rose in the opening scene of *Aggression,* where it symbolized ideal love.

Here the hands are bound by chains; ideal love is a binding from which one cannot escape. This contrast between the desire to be free, and the desire to be bound, indeed, chained to another, in ideal love, is at the center of Violetta's complex feelings in the aria and a major theme in the film.

After the film's dramatic opening, we are plunged into the world of opera, where scenes from Verdi's *La Rigoletto* are played out, and where love is problematized, and often results in death. We see Magdalena Montezuma as Therese Neuman, stigmata bearing woman, who on the first day of Lent, March 5, 1926, said that she developed a wound above her heart. At first, she didn't tell anyone. But as the blood began to show through her clothing, she could no longer hide the fact. There has been some controversy surrounding her claim, but the important thing is that her story involves a mystical event and her attempt to keep it secret. Violetta also keeps her emotions secret as does Gilda in *Rigoletto* and Carlo, who keeps the secret that he is gay from his father.

In the following scene, we see the martyrdom of Saint Sebastian, his suffering and death. In gay culture, Sebastian has stood for a homosexual ideal, with his physique, naked except for a loincloth, and pierced by arrows, suggesting penetration. But his suffering can also be interpreted as a kind of internalized pain caused by being in the closet about his sexuality. Montezuma plays Saint Irene of Rome, who, in the original story rescued and healed Sebastian. In this story, he would die a violent death later in his life. In Schroeter's film, Sebastian dies and is carried on a board by Irene and two other women. I can't help seeing a resonance between Sebastian here and Jesus Christ, between Irene and the Virgin Mary. In fact, later in the film, Schroeter will show a statue of the Virgin Mary with her arms extended over Rome. Schroeter, as I have noted earlier, did not see a contradiction in his use of Catholic iconography and his homosexuality, though he was, in his last film, *Deux,* highly critical of the Church.

Then we see Montezuma in drag, a tragic figure, dancing with Carla who is more extroverted. Montezuma dances behind her. She continues her exuberant, stylized, unabashed, and
improvisatory manner of dancing. At one point, she stretches
her arm forward and flicks her wrist as she turns it; as she goes
through this motion, she smiles and looks at the camera, as if
she and Schroeter had a good laugh at her queer gesture. It is
a charming moment in the film, and you have to be paying attention otherwise you'll miss it. Intercut with these scenes of
Magdalena and Carla dancing, in what we realize later in the
film is a gay bar, are scenes that dramatize the death of Siegfried
(Sigurd Salto) and his being mourned by Kriemhild (Magdalena
Montezuma); these scenes are excerpted from the Nibelungen
myth.[1] Montezuma exhibits her grief at his death, moving her
hands slowly over his body, and in a series of stylized movements of her arms, expresses her extreme despair. During this
scene, we hear the great opera singer Rosa Ponselle, singing "Tu
che Invoco," from Spotini's rarely performed opera, *La Vestale*
(The Vestal). In the opera, Julia, the vestal, is wrongly accused
of being promiscuous, convicted, and sentenced to the terrible
death of being buried alive. The High Priest and Vestal Priestess
release her, after a supernatural occurrence, and she is allowed
to marry the man whom she loved. Julia, like Violetta, struggled
to hide her feelings; in the former case, because Julia belonged
to the order of the Vestal virgins, and in the latter, because Violetta wanted to preserve her sexual freedom. Carla, on the other
hand, is playful, and uninhibited, a figure of freedom.

Carla and Montezuma are lesbian lovers. In one scene, Montezuma winds Carla up as though she were a doll; she moves her
body wildly, as if she were a mechanical doll, as we "The Mad
Scene" from Act 4 of Ambrose Thomas's opera, *Hamlet,* sung by
an uncredited singer. Perhaps, Montezuma is gaslighting Carla,

---

1   In the Nibelungen myth, Siegfied falls in love with Kriemhild without hav-
     ing seen her and woos her from a distance. He goes on many adventures in
     his search for her. Finally, he meets her and they are married. But having
     been accused of sleeping with Brunhild, he is killed by Hagen, a fierce war-
     rior. Kriemhild vows revenge.

or her show of freedom is for madness. Soon, Carla seems as if she has been released from Montezuma's control. The theme of control and freedom was introduced in *Neurasia,* but here it is developed to its conclusion on two levels.

One narrative shows Carla in a relationship with a man and another, interwoven with that one, shows her leaving with Magdalena on a train. In the first narrative, she grows old and dies. That is the heterosexual narrative. In the other narrative, Carla leaves with her lover, Magdalena. Schroeter inserts a voiceover as Carla, dressed elegantly, is saying her goodbyes to friends:

> In this very moment I realized that my life from now on was totally meaningless. All my plans, expectations, and all my aims were lost. They disappeared with the world which had given them their sense. This moment was of complete loneliness and despair. If I had to complain about the loss of any relatives or friends, it might have been mortal but …vanity which had occasionally marked my former life now turned out to be helpful. There was nobody expected anything from me. Strange, my feelings were not at all loneliness and despair but almost something like deliverance and freedom. From now on I was my own master; no longer a tiny wheel in the big machinery of life. Let it be a world of terror and dangerous paths which I had to discover. I'll conquer it in my own way; no longer a slave of strange and unrecognized forces and operations, which I don't understand and which don't touch me at all.

These words begin when Carla and Montezuma are leaving the bar; there is some tension between them, suggesting the mechanical doll incident. Carla seems alternately happy and sad. Perhaps she is sad about having to leave. We do not know the reason. On the platform, Carla is saying goodbye to a man. She is leaving the heterosexual world. But if the voiceover refers to Carla's feeling about leaving, then we realize that she accepts the potential danger: "Let it be a world of terror and dangerous paths." At this point, the scene on the train is intercut with scenes of Carla in her former life as a wife. But now she feels something almost like "freedom and deliverance." Ultimately, the world as she saw it disappeared and now, she has to re-define her world.

The two narratives seem to merge and complicate themselves with the introduction of the song, "Love is a Golden Ring," sung by Frankie Lane, with the lines: "Love is forever a rare and lasting thing / Love is a golden ring / A wedding in the church / The happiness and tears / The little ring you'll wear / Will last through all the years / And in our golden days / We'll find eternal spring…" The song's lyrics and the voiceover contrast with each other. One speaks of eternal love, symbolized by the ideal rose, and the other of "freedom and deliverance." Frankie Lane begins singing at the moment when Carla is slowly letting go of her husband's hand. The train moves slowly down the track, gathering speed, as the song continues. The song is ironic, in that it refers to a world that Carla and Montezuma are leaving behind. That is at least is one interpretation. But Schroeter is ambiguous here. Perhaps the song is meant for Carla and Montezuma. The two narratives, existing, as if, in two alternate realities now come together and clash. Has Violetta abandoned her aria or not? Has she embraced Alfredo? The film is indecisive at this point.

In the next sequences in the film, Schroeter presents various dramatic and stylized performances of scenes from Verdi's *Rigoletto*. Montezuma plays the hunchbacked jester, Rigoletto, "in a cross-dressing part reminiscent of queer German cinema of the Weimer period…whose daughter ends up sacrificing her life in a web of intrigues involving her father and the lecherous Duke for whom he works." In the scene where the Duke of Mantua, speaking of the frailty of human fame and material things, is professing his love to Gilda, we see the courtiers, lurking to the left of the screen and gazing upon the enraptured lovers. At one point, there is a cut, and we see a close up of Sigurd Salto, who played Sebastian, in civilian clothes, seeming as though he is hurt or exhausted and about to fall, in medium close-up. Finally, he falls to ground, apparently dead. Inserting this scene in the

sequence of the opera, collapses art and life. The music of Rigoletto is interrupted, and we hear a series of random sounds. We
are suddenly in a different space, or perhaps, a parallel space,
which is sinister. An elegantly dressed woman has shot and
killed a man in a courtyard; his very drawn out, exaggerated
movements as he's dying, is typical of Schroeter's dramatic techniques. This is an inversion, perhaps, of the scene in *Tosca* where
Cavordissi is actually killed by the firing squad; here, a woman
kills a man. Inserting this scene in the sequence of the opera,
collapses art and life. Life is a kind of performance on a stage, a
mock performance; the woman points the gun, but it does not
go off; there is no blood in the scene. It is drama, theatre, and
there is no attempt by Schroeter to simulate real life. He is fundamentally not a realist but a mannerist.

We see a medium shot of Salto, standing in front of a factory.
Then, the camera moves closer, and settles on a medium close
up of Salto's face. We begin to hear the lovely sounds of Maria
Strada's voice singing the "Et Incarnatus Est" part from Mozart's
Mass in C minor; the phrase comes from the Credo, in Christian
liturgy: "et incarnatus est de spiritu sancto ex Maria virgine, et
homo factus est" ("He was incarnate by the Holy Spirit from the
Virgin Mary and was made man"). Indeed, the camera lovingly
caresses Salto's face, and this particular use of Mozart's music
suggests a connection here between Salto and Christ/Sebastian.
During this scene, we also see Salto, in pain, leaning against a
tree, and falling to the ground. Then, a medium close up of the
elegant woman, holding the gun. As Mozart's music stops, we
hear the sound of thunder mixed with what sounds like industrial noise and see the elegant woman and the man embracing
as they are walking on a street. He is now alive. Schroeter has reversed the time sequence. Or perhaps these are alternative realities. Soon both their bodies are wracked by pain, as if the harsh
industrial sounds have killed them.

There is another way in which Schroeter creates two alternate
realities in the film: by using the double. Salto, a blonde, and
the dark-haired man are both wearing a blue scarf which links
them in a sequence; we can see them as doubles; the dark-haired

man is shot and killed. In another scene, he is manhandled by a stranger and left on the ground, wounded. Salto is then seen, in the rain, with his body in pain. If we think of the double here, it is as if Salto feels the man's pain. On the soundtrack there is the distorted sound of bombs exploding; a reference to the war and the bombing of Germany in 1945. It also suggests the increasing power of the military in post war Germany. The film is becoming darker and the harsh sounds of the real world are beginning to intrude on the mythic space. Now the figures in the film must learn to survive.

Both Salto and the dark-haired man are struggling to exist in a world increasing dominated by industry and capitalism: "Life is very precious, even right now." Those were Carla's final words, and they are a testament "to the queer spirit of survival." Scenes of factories, power plants, the sounds of traffic and police whistles, continue to dominate and invade the screen. In reaction to this, we are suddenly thrust into the *Tosca* sequence. As with *Rigoletto,* Schroeter "presents key moments of the text out of order (the segment starts with Tosca's suicide) and emphasizes the topics he deems most important — in this case, not Tosca's love for Cavaradossi, who is executed, but her relationship to Scarpia, whom she kills personally." He chooses those excerpts as a commentary on the images.

In the final scene of the opera, Tosca tells Cavaradossi to play dead when the firing squad shoots at him with blanks. He tells her, without any fear, that he will act "like Tosca in the theatre." She exclaims "Ecco un artista!" ("What an actor!"), after the soldiers finish shooting and Cavaradossi falls down. But Tosca has been tricked by Scarpia since the bullets were, in fact, real. The way Schroeter shoots the sequence in the film is brilliant. Montezuma utilizes all her skill as an actress; she paces nervously at first, as the firing squad begins to aim; after the guns go off, and he falls to the ground, she folds her hands briefly, with a smile on her face, believing she is successful in her plot and that he is not dead. She moves closer and closer, and then when she realizes he is dead, she clasps her face, with both hands, in horror. The subtle way in which Montezuma modulates her movements, gives the scene a feeling of great tension; she manages to subtly evoke her shifting emotions. Schroeter is able to bring something new and unique to a scene that every opera aficionado knows by heart. The final scene was also intercut with scenes of people carrying Sebastian's body. The cuts between Sebastian and Tosca's lover link the religious martyrdom of the former with the profane death of the latter, and ultimately display a tragic vision of the world.

We are now suddenly plunged into a domestic scene, involving a father and son. They are seated a table in a small kitchen. The father is angry at his son, Carlo. He complains, in a Neapolitan dialect (the film has no subtitles), at his son's indifference, and says that he only thinks of himself and does nothing to help his mother or his father. Carlo is silent. After a few minutes, he leaves. The scene then cuts to Carlo and another young man, Mario. Carlo has an erection. The man across from him feigns indifference, while casually glancing at Carlo's pants, and then looking away. Carlo is seduced. In the next few scenes, they are seen walking around the city streets holding hands and sitting down on the grass in a park and talk. At one point, they slowly and casually cross a street full of traffic, weaving through the individual cars. All this is happening with a background of noisy traffic, and industrial buildings and factories. We are no longer in the aesthetic space of opera and myth.

We then return to the kitchen and the father again complains that Carlo does nothing, suggesting he is a bum. But now Mario sits next to him. The father says, "My son, don't you see that you can't go away with this stranger? He'll abandon you, it will be the end of you, you must stay here." The young men are silent, indifferent, and look away from Carlo's father. They leave but the father decides to follow them. Soon he discovers his dead son lying on the Riviera di Chiaia. Looking over this scene is a statue of Jesus with his arms open. Life mirrors art, and like in the operas, love concludes with death. In the following scenes of Mario travelling to Capri in order to transport Carlo's body,

Schroeter lengthens the time of the shots and in doing so, creates a sense of timelessness.

As we see Mario in a medium shot setting out for Capri to lay Mario's body to rest, we hear the voice of Elisabeth Schwarzkopf singing the song "Im Abendrot" (In the glow of evening) by Richard Strauss, one of his last songs. Mario's hair is blowing in the wind, as we see the city receding and the wide-open sea churning under the boat's motor, on the left of the screen. In the distance, a ship moves slowly across the ocean. It is one of the most brilliant sustained scenes in the film. It is composed of a single shot that lasts over ten minutes, and that exemplifies "queer art's non-normative perception of time. The slow, drawn-out character" of this scene, as well as the scene in Capri where Mario handles Carlo's dead body, "reference a mythological timelessness that sidesteps normal concepts of time." At one point, Mario thinks of Carlo, and Schroeter cuts to a close up of he and Carlo gazing into each other's eyes. The lyrics to Strauss's song are the following:

> How lovely is your world,
> Father, in its golden radiance
> when your glory descends
> and paints the dust with glitter;
> when the red light that shines from the clouds
> falls silently upon my window.
> Could I complain? Could I be apprehensive?
> Could I lose faith in you and in myself?
> No, I already bear your heaven
> here within my heart.
> And this heart, before it breaks,
> still drinks in the fire and savors the light.

This scene is "reminiscent of queer filmmaker Gregory Markopoulos's depiction of New York Harbor in *Twice a Man* (1963), and demonstrates the influence of American underground film on Schroeter." As we see Mario, at Capri, motioning toward the sky, with upraised hands, we hear again Callas singing the

"Sempre Libera" from *La Traviata*. As the aria speaks of sexual freedom, the use of it may appear ironic. It contrasts with the solemnity of Strauss. But the aria is abruptly cut and then we hear the voice of Carlo's father expressing agony over his son's death while the statue of Jesus appears on the screen. We have seen the way in which Schroeter has associated love with death and religion with martyrdom. Art has collapsed into life. The death of Carlo mirrored the death of Violetta. In a different sense, high and low art achieve a kind of symbiosis that is extraordinary in Schroeter's cinema.

Suddenly, the scene changes back to the beginning of the film, with Gisela Trowe as the aging prostitute in Verdi's opera. We have come full circle. The dramatic scenes that follow show Alfredo and Violetta expressing love for each other and these are intercut with Callas singing the "Sempra Libera" aria.[2] The tension is between love and freedom. Violetta's dilemma is that she wants to love but is afraid of giving up her freedom. When she realizes that she is not afraid anymore, and that the pain and discomfort have left her, she dies. She is transformed in death, and we are reminded of the *Liebestod* of Wagner's Isolde. In *The Death of Maria Malibran*, Schroeter will develop this idea much further. Throughout the scenes with Violetta, we see a flickering candle in the background. This "allegorizes the cruelties that attach themselves to the passing of time in a patriarchal culture that treats women like mere tools and objects."

After the *La Traviata* sequence, Schroeter concludes the film with a sequence composed of prior scenes from the film, but this is not repetition; he uses alternate takes, with different camera angles. It is a kind of theme and variation, a fitting conclusion to a film that is itself constructed like a large musical composition. We see Saint Irene in despair and Sebastian tied to the tree; Salto in front of a factory or power plant; Theresa Newman; the dark haired man being beat up in the street; a statue of

---

2 During this sequence of excerpts from *La Traviata*, Schroeter used the recording of an aria from the opera that Maria Cebotari sang on Reich Radio in 1943. That is why you hear Verdi's opera sung in German.

the Virgin Mary; and then we hear Carla's words, "Life is very precious, even right now." Schroeter also uses, during this final sequence, the pop song, "Save the Last Dance for Me," which is about a lover's plea to the one she loves, even though he flirts with others, that at the end of the night he'll come home with her. During the song, the narrator becomes increasing desperate, and demands that her lover tell anyone who approaches him that he is hers alone. It is a song about obsessive love. This is followed by the song by Frankie Lane, "Love Is a Golden Ring," a song about ideal love, where "love is a forever rare and lasting thing." This sequence, that comes at the end of the film, does have a tongue and cheek quality, and yet it highlights the central conflict in the film, between ideal love and the limits it puts on individual freedom. Of course, the difference between "Love is a golden ring" and "Save the Last Dance for me" is between the finality of marriage and obsessive love.

Schroeter also wittily films himself directing the man who played Mario. Midway during this scene we hear the very last piece of music in the film. It is an excerpt from Lenora's aria, "D'amor sull'all rosee" from the fourth act of Verdi's *Il Trovatore*, sung by Celestine Boninsegna. Here is the excerpt that Schroeter uses:

Com'aura di Speranza [Like a breeze of hope]
Allegia in quella stanza: [linger in that room]
Lo desta alle memorie, [wake him up to remembrance]
Ai sogni dell'amor! [To dreams of love!]
Ma deh! Non dirgi improvvido, [Yet do not imprudently]
Le pene del moi cor! [reveal the woes of my heart]

As we see Schroeter's hand on the young man's shoulder, we hear the beginning of the aria. Then we see Mario on the boat, on his way to Capri, as we hear the beginning of the fourth line "Ai sogni"; the rest of that line, "dell'amor" is sung while a photo of Maria Callas looking pensive is on the screen. As Boninsegna hits a high note, improvising on the words "immrovvido" and "le penne," we see a photo of Maria Callas as if in drag. The high note stands for exuberance, as well as hysterical despair, and is a characteristic pleasure for connoisseurs of opera. The final image on the screen is of Callas in a pensive mood. Here the phrase "le pene del mio cor" is sung and as it is being repeated, Schroeter ends the film with the word "pene," meaning "woes." By excerpting these words, out of context, Schroeter is able to generate an additional layer of meaning to the images on the screen. *Eika Katappa* began with Violetta's aria "sempera libera" about her desire to be sexually free, which is interrupted by Alfredo's will to love her. In the aria from *Il Trovatore,* Lenora is willing to exchange herself for her lover, who is in prison, in order to free him from the Count. But Lenora takes poison in order to remain faithful to him, and so as not to give herself to the Count. Love culminates in death in both operas. The two last lines of the aria from *Il Trovatore* speak of keeping one's pain a secret. But Silence = Death. *Eika Katappa,* is also about queer survival: "Life is very precious, even now." There has been a rise in attacks on the gay, lesbian, and trans community in recent years. But even after all the violence and hatred, it is important never to forget that life is precious and worth fighting for. Schroeter's empathy is clear behind the film. In 1969, the film was awarded the Josef von Sternberg Prize at the Mannheim Film Festival. In his autobiography, Schroeter writes that having won the prize, "represented a rebellion against ordinary narrative drama in the cinema."

Works Cited

Grundmann, Roy. "The Passions of Werner Schroeter." In *Werner Schroeter,* ed. Roy Grundmann, 2–56. Vienna: Österreichisches Filmmuseum; Synema-Gesellschaft für Film und Medien, 2018.

Schroeter, Werner, and Claudia Lenssen. *Days of Twilight, Nights of Frenzy.* Translated by Anthea Bell. Chicago: University of Chicago Press, 2017.

THE SEVENTIES *and* EIGHTIES

Stylized Realism

5

The Unfolding of Desire:
On Werner Schroeter's *Der Bomberpilot*

Isn't every work of art, every artistic creation, yet another attempt
to cancel out the unbearable nature of reality? An attempt to take
reality off its hinges, by an act of yearning. Artists and anarchists
are united in refusing to submit to what is intolerable in the
world as it exists.

— Werner Schroeter

The first image in Werner Schroeter's absurdist comedy, *Der Bomberpilot* (The Bomber Pilot) (1970), is of a hand waving a flag on which there is a swastika, in front of a kind of majestic building all in white, with many steps, and we realize that this is Nazi Germany; later we will find out that this is the period near the end of the war. From the right of the screen our three female protagonists, Mascha, Carla, and Magdalena, emerge, in a stylized dance movement, going toward the left side of the screen, smiling at the camera and waving their hands, as if to say goodbye, each wearing corsets and garter belts. They represent the lives of the common people under National Socialism. The erotic power of their presence, their smiles, their sense of indifference to their surroundings, undercuts the seriousness of the Nazi flag and the Nazi ideal of womanly beauty. Even their Nazi salutes are merely performative, and they seem to lack any genuine feeling for or alliance with Nazi Germany. The scene is almost absurd. We eventually come to see how their desire and longing come into conflict with institutional thinking, the administrative horror that was Nazi Germany.

They search for employment, for a way to fulfill their desires under the Reich. Mascha and Magdalena visit an employment office. Magdalena asks for an administrative position and gestures to a medal she is wearing which she says she received in World War I and that entitles her to a good position in society. Mascha is shy and unsure of herself and asks for work in a retirement home for dogs, though Magdalena insists Mascha could also work in nursing. The woman at the employment office who is interviewing them seems almost shocked at their requests for such positions and is indifferent to their desires: the institution is fundamentally against desire. Mascha will eventually suffer depression and a mental breakdown and end up as a "beauty dancer." There are some highly romantic and beautiful images of her dancing in a forest with a laurel or a kind of wig made from flowers on her head; here she attempts to express her desire but at the same time, we are told that she is part of a "free-spirted performance group" that forces her to dance early in the morning. Magdalena will be employed as a restorer of old religious paintings. Neither is fully able to express their desires without some restriction or within a kind of disciplined environment. This is their life in Nazi Germany.

Carla, who is separated from the two women at this point in the film (they will reunite late during a concert of Bruckner's music), dreams of singing a part in a Viennese tragedy. She is in love with the sentimental songs that were popular in the 40s such as Strauss's Viennese waltz, "Wiener Blut (Viennese Spirit)." During the day, she works in a bakery shop. One morning, a young man comes into the shop, played by Werner Schroeter himself, who is shy and withdrawn, and who expresses his love for her by giving her a bundle of flowers. In the very next scene, intercut with scenes of the young man and Carla in a boat enjoying the summer weather as they glide on the water, we see a woman frantically running into the bakery (soon we will realize why: the young man was hit by a car and has died). Then we see Carla rushing to him and holding onto his dead body lying across the front of a car, scattered flowers at his side. This is the first of Carla's tragic disappointments in life and there will be others as she seeks to create a life for herself in Nazi Germany. Love is not possible in such a bleak world.

There is a sequence in the film where we are given a glimpse into Mascha's emotional state and which highlights Schroeter's unique use of image and sound. At the beginning of the scene she is composed, with an expression of longing and disgust on her face. Suddenly, she becomes animated, gesticulating wildly, expressing pent up rage, and we hear on the soundtrack words like "death and beauty," which suggest the Nazi ideal of masculine beauty and their cult of death. But the soundtrack is not synched with the movements of her mouth. Such effects are typical of Schroeter's early films. Here, the intense longing and frustration that are expressed seems to fight against the very restrictions of the cinematic screen; the words spoken are something other than what is expressed through physical movement, and do not reveal so much as they obscure what is being felt and can only be shown. Thus, the words are out of synch with the movements of her mouth. This is also a rejection of the idea of professional acting, and of realism in cinema. Later, in the scenes where the women are singing in a variety performance for GIs in America this will become apparent; they sing off key and the words are out of synch with the movements of the mouth; this is also a rejection of the idea of the "perfect performance." What is important is desire and longing, expressed with intensity, not any considerations about whether a performance is "good" or "bad." It is the feeling that counts, and the physical intensity with which the feeling is expressed; in this respect there is no difference between these singers and Maria Callas. Schroeter is a mannerist; gestures are performative and do not reveal any psychological truth about the women; their gestures are exaggerated, self-conscious, overblown, exhibiting a desire that overwhelms and can barely be articulated.

After the collapse of Germany, the women decide they must go to America[1]; they speak of showing support for oppressed women, and the need to unite under feminism; after smoking a "filtered marijuana cigarette" they become enlightened, so to speak, and decide to end racial segregation. During this sequence, where the women are smoking a joint during breakfast, Schroeter inserts a brief scene of the women in the company of an African American man and woman. The whole sequence is somewhat humorous and absurd but not without a touch of irony. Of course, May 1968 was still fresh in many people's minds when Schroeter made this film and the Leftist revolutions in the '70s would eventually degenerate into terrorism and murder: think of the RAF in Germany and Red Faction in Italy. Schroeter is not interested in conventional politics; and yet his provocative expression of a Leftist sensibility can cause a viewer to think about the possibilities of how these ideas can be embodied in the real world. In these present times, when we see the world swinging to the Right, I think Schroeter's films are absolutely essential in rethinking our essential freedoms. For Schroeter, desire and passion must lead the way. One must remember that Schroeter is not a realist but a mannerist. For him the drama and theatricality of life is more important than the straight and narrow path.

In America, the women want to use "their influence as teachers" (they pay a visit to the school that Schroeter attended as a child) but eventually they are "suspected of being communists," and their "credibility [is] undermined." They realize that their "idealized view of racial integration foundered in the face of the myriad of foreign realities." Finally, Mascha's affair with a bomber pilot puts an end to their residence in America. Dur-

---

1   Before they decide to go to America, Carla says: "I can only think back to the successes of 1943, to the Viennese operetta, with the choirboys. It was simply fantastic." Mascha tells Carla, "You're too fixed in the past. We must unite with all the women who are oppressed."

ing the legal proceedings that followed, the fact that they were German did not work in their favor. Such demonizing of immigrants is sadly common even today. Here, Schroeter suggests that America is no different from Germany in terms of the way they treat common people and immigrants.

Near the conclusion of the film, the women create a variety show for American officers: Mascha sings a song by Richard Wagner about the transformative nature of sorrow, Carla, dressed in a sailor's outfit, sings a song about loss, and Magdalena, performs the "snake dance," with the tattoo of a snake across her neck with its mouth open, ready to bite. The song that accompanies Magdalena is by Yma Sumac, the Peruvian coloratura, and her performance is an intense embodiment of primitive forces. This is followed by a dance performance by all three women, which appears completely improvised and free; they seem in a kind of trance, giving full voice to the complexity of their desires as German women. They sing a song from Franz Lehar's operetta, *Giuditta,* that they once performed in Nazi Germany, with lines like "I dance in a trance" and "my lips give kisses so torrid" and with the refrain, "you should kiss / you should love." Such intense feeling is the driving force in Schroeter's films. But in another sense, "the cabaret is really a showcase of degraded fragments": the performance of Wagner, the B-movie "snake dance," and the sailor songs are really "degraded fragments of hegemonic culture that actually fail to add up to a great synthesis," i.e., Wagner's concept of the *Gesamtkunstwerk,* or the total work of art.[2] Schroeter is against the idea of a totality and is an artist who is working with the fragments of a decaying culture. I am reminded of Walter Benjamin's idea of the filmic medium, "as an explosive device capable of shattering the prison of alienated industrial modernity, 'so that now, in the midst of its far-flung ruins and debris, we calmly and adventurously go travelling.'" For Caryl Flinn, the injection of "materi-

---

2 Wagner used this term to mean a comprehensive work of art which employed all the means at its disposal, in terms of the music and visuals, in order to produce a kind of grand spectacle.

alized kitsch" is also a kind of homeopathic treatment, where, "what happens is less a control over undesirable aspects of the past than a momentary embrace, *a way of bringing them into relationship with our present identity.*" In this respect, *Der Bomberpilot* is about exorcising of the demons of the past through destroying the sense of a total synthesis, which is an aspect of hegemonic culture, and through working with and transforming the degraded fragments of a culture in ruin. And in this they satirize the concept of the strong Aryan woman; they are not disciplined or good German women. They are unemployed and without bank accounts or bourgeois responsibilities.

The songs that the women sing throughout the film suggest an amateurism which Schroeter identifies with a Utopian vision. Roy Grundmann, in his essay on Schroeter's film, *Poussières d'amour* (Love's Debris), writes, speaking of Roland Barthes: "According to Barthes, what characterizes the amateur is not the devout enthusiasm obtained by listening to a professional, but the irrepressible urge to make music. Amateurism is defined by a certain style more than by imperfection." Furthermore, "The possibility of being disappointed is the factor that makes hope what it is in the first place — utopian — and also grounds it in reality. The disappointment of hope is unconditional. It lets hope 'open in a forward…future-oriented direction; it does not address itself to that which already exists.'" The women exhibit an inner strength despite their circumstances. But Schroeter is also commenting on the history of cinema in those scenes where the soundtrack is out of synch with the movements of the mouth. Often one gets the sense, despite the soundtrack, that one is watching a silent film; the gestures are so pronounced and excessive, so theatrical and self-conscious, that one is witnessing those qualities that normally characterize a silent film. The detachment of the soundtrack with the voice also draws attention to the artificial quality of sound in films.

In another respect, the music in Schroeter's films also acts as commentary and ironic counterpoint to the images. During the scene where Mascha is helping Magdalena from a river after her suicide attempt (following the scene that announces Germany has lost the war), and trying to resuscitate her, we hear Caterina Valente (one of Schroeter's favorite singers next to Callas) singing her 1954 song, "Schwarze Engel" (Black Angel) with the lyrics: "Why do you never think / That an angel can be black?," "Whether we are rich or poor / We will all die," and "That shows we're all the same / When we stand at heaven's door." When they return to their apartment, Magdalena screams, "Sold out, Sold out," "I know…strong," "Die…" and "I have an injury." She is criticizing herself because she feels at this point that she has not lived up to the Nazi ideals of strength and its cult of death and beauty. Furthermore, Grundmann writes, "Schroeter misses no opportunity to turn *Der Bomberpilot* into a comical record of their [the women's] conceits, failures, and what one may call a salutary ineptitude to be efficient Nazi women." The song is ironic in the sense that Magdalena does not realize yet the fundamental truth that "we're all the same" and "whether rich or poor / we will all die." Schroeter is a master at the use of music in conjunction with images; meanings overlap and resonate creating a complex visual and auditory experience in the viewer.

These out of synch sequences also draw attention to the performative quality of drag: the crude and imperfect quality of the singing voice that characterizes a typical drag performance, where excess destabilizes any sense of realism. The voice is disembodied and this disjunct between image and sound also suggests gender performance, where the voice and the image play with the idea of gender. Schroeter's cinematic image and soundtrack enact in a visual/auditory space the experience of a transvestite: the initially awkward performance of gender, the disjunct between a voice and image before it becomes normalized and the problems and complexity of gender are reduced, in other words, before the transvestite has undergone a sex-change operation. And this is a hallmark of Schroeter's visual and auditory style, given in its rawest form in *Der Bomberpilot*. Furthermore, concerning the "disembodied voice," Roy Grundmann writes:

The disembodied female voice is a central feature of Schroeter's use of sound in many of his films. It is a mark of his fragmented aesthetics, but can more specifically be related to the phenomenon of the disembodied voice that is valorized by feminists for eluding the semantic constraints of the patriarchal symbolic.[3]

With Schroeter's wide ranging use of music, from jazz to popular music and opera, and the theatrical and stylized gestures of the actors, one gets the sense of an excess, born of his complex use of image and sound, which destabilizes our sense of the cinematic image and its function. It is almost more than the screen can bear; it explodes the codes of a male-dominated culture. It contains within it the history of film while being critical of all that a typical image is supposed to do, that is, reproduce a feeling of reality for popular consumption i.e. the typical Hollywood film.

Schroeter also plays with gender roles in his audio and visual style in another way. One of the most brilliant, characteristic and subtle close ups in the film occurs after Carla, wearing a sailor's outfit, has finishing singing her song about loss. Here, it is as if Carla has changed genders through a trick of framing and light. She is transformed into a young sailor with an expression on "his" face of desire and longing, and with a seductive pose, even after she has sung this song about loss. Schroeter captures his/her erotic expression brilliantly; it is the magic of his cinema. Even in the face of failure, the fire of passion is not quenched; failure only exists to give character to an inner strength that persists in the face of tragedy. This is something Schroeter himself knew well. Grundmann writes, "Keenly aware of the inevitability of failure and tragedy, Schroeter never allowed his awareness to quell his stubborn sense of hope in the face of more reasonable-sounding calls for pragmatism and efficiency — values that, as we already saw, [Herbert] Mar-

---

3   One can also see the use of the "disembodied voice" in much contemporary experimental poetry as well as its "fragmentary quality."

cuse identifies as central to the performance principle." Here, "performance principle" suggests a professional, perfect performance. The women are most "themselves" when performing on stage, giving free reign to their complex desires, and for Schroeter, this shows his faith in the transformative nature of artistic performance and its power to heal.

There is an important scene early in the film, with Magdalena, where Schroeter distinguishes between mannerism and realism in photography; it is the closest to a kind of manifesto in Schroeter's films. At one point in the film, Magdalena receives "a post teaching adult education for the Reich," to "discuss the problem of mannerism in modernity as it relates to photography." She has brought a book that contains photos of the opera singer Elisabeth Schwarzkopf. She examines three photos, and we get a crash course in Nazi aesthetics and modern art. As she speaks about the first photo, the soundtrack of her voice is out of synch with the movements of her mouth which suggests that she is self-conscious and insincere:

> In a most indirect way, an expression of great tension has been captured on the artist's face. It is a document of humanity. Notice how even the composition of the photo emphasizes the artist's expression of exhaustion and happiness after a performance.

Notice the emphasis on humanity; the irony, of course, is that this scene occurs during the Third Reich. Magdalena continues:

> In contrast to that we have a bad photo on page 2. A portrait. There everything is posed. The lighting emphasizes the extreme artificiality of the position of her head and the assured, knowing, soulful glance upward seems insincere. That example shows that photography as a representational medium can only produce the insincerity and artificiality of expression.

As opposed to the emphasis on exhaustion, happiness, and humanity in the first photo, the second photo is in the mannerist style close to Schroeter's own aesthetics. The book speaks of the problem of photography as a "representational medium" when speaking of a mannerist photo and thus it stands for a criticism of modern art in general. Of course, the realism of those paintings that were popular during the time of the Reich stand in opposition to modern art. Finally, there is a third photo, which is closest to the ideal of a Nazi aesthetics: "Finally, let us look at the singer at ease among her family on page 15. Here nothing is posed. We see Elizabeth Schwarzkopf with her dog. Here we see the beautiful side of photography, because here it is human." Again, the ironic emphasis on humanity during the Third Reich. The immediate scene after this one announces that the Germans have fallen in the war and shows Magdalena attempting suicide by drowning. Even though Schroeter's later films were influenced by Italian neo-realism, he was never strictly a political filmmaker or a realist in the conventional sense and never lost sight of his mannerist style. Grundmann, in his essay, "The Passions of Werner Schroeter," writes:

> It is precisely Schroeter's distance from organized activism that shaped his own politics. Instead of using cinema for political manifestos or retreating into the formal orthodoxy of political modernism, Schroeter's militancy consisted of elevating the personal to the political in a consequential manner. One may call him an anarchist of the imagination. The comparison to anarchism, with its valorization of radical heterogeneity, its distrust of organized politics of any kind, and its interest in ritualistic performance and alternative base cultures, is by no mean far-fetched.

In this respect, Carla, Marsha, and Magdalena's lives are elevated to the political through the various choices they have made.

The very last scene of the film shows Magdalena helping Carla, because of an injury to her hip. As they walk, Carla is no longer youthful and walks with great difficulty. Magdalena is also a bit older. Life for those common German people after the war was extremely difficult. These women attempted to transform their bleak lives through artistic performance. There is a moment of redemption but it is transitory. Life intercedes and the result is tragic for Carla. A man was behind it; the bomber pilot of the title, who appears briefly in the film. Schroeter simply had his actresses walk alongside and engage with American soldiers he found while visiting the US. Then Schroeter filmed Marsha with one of them and the soldier thus became the bomber pilot of the film. The bomber pilot was initially involved with Mascha before his affair with Carla that resulted in her miscarriage. And so, the bomber pilot is directly connected to the tragedy that befalls Carla and by extension all the women. The film ends on a somber note.

Desire, the passionate expression of feeling, the physicality of performance, these are the central qualities in Schroeter's early films, and they are seen in their rawest form in *Der Bomberpilot*; these qualities stand in opposition to the institutionalization of life through capitalism, which kills the dreamer who imagines an alternate mode of existence. Mascha, Carla, and Magdalena seek employment but without success. Only Carla holds on to her dream of being a singer which will eventually prove tragic when she is impregnated by Mascha's bomber pilot and suffers a miscarriage that damages her hip. Life is a killer. In reference to the women's desire, I kept thinking of Debord's notion of *dérive,* a drift or drifting, "behaving in a playful and productive manner, all of which is quite different from classic notions of a journey or stroll." This is the motion of desire, which does not follow a straight and narrow path, but is open to improvisations, and remains essentially open-ended. These three women attempt to earn their "right to live" through finding jobs, but they suffer displacement rather than any sense of security. Schroeter sympathizes with them. These women are artists but not the bourgeois type.

Der Bomberpilot is one Schroeter's key early films. It shows the plight of common people under National Socialism and afterwards as they try to rebuild their lives in America. In the film, the women use their erotic power and the physicality of performance to project their desires; offkey and "bad" singing become the alternative to professionalism and the ideal performance; the soundtrack, out of sync with the movements of the voice, is Schroeter's provocative way of criticizing the cinematic image and the use of a soundtrack and destabilizing the viewer's expectations of what a film should do. Mannerism is a rejection of the realism which Schroeter sees as the benchmark of Nazi aesthetics; he has said that he hates documentaries. Carla, Mascha, and Magdalena exhibit strength in following their own desires, after having failed to secure employment. Such a trajectory of desire is filled with disappointments and tragedy, but there is a moment of freedom, near the end of the film, when they are dancing together, improvising, as if drifting rather than following measured steps. Schroeter relishes the scene, filming them from various angles, and using closeups, to frame their physical movements, in what is essentially a trance-like and erotic experience for the women, one that undercuts the sense of hopelessness in the ending of the film. It shows that desire is possible in such a bleak world, and that healing is also possible, providing enough for hope to survive. *Der Bomberpilot* is one of Schroeter's most important and powerful early films; it is an absurdist comedy that provokes us into rethinking the uses of sound and image in film and their relation to revolutionary desire.

Works Cited

Debord, Guy. "La dérive." Translated by Jonathan Simons. *The Analog Sea Review* 2 (2019): 104–8.

Flinn, Caryl. *New German Cinema: Music, Memory, and the Matter of Style.* Berkeley: University of California Press, 2003.

Grundmann, Roy. "A Quivering Tremor, a Vibration in Space: Voicing Utopia in *Poussières d'amour*." In *Werner Schroeter,* ed. Roy Grundmann, 159–77. Vienna: Österreichisches Filmmuseum; Synema-Gesellschaft für Film und Medien, 2018.

———. "The Passions of Werner Schroeter." In *Werner Schroeter,* ed. Roy Grundmann, 2–56. Vienna: Österreichisches Filmmuseum; Synema-Gesellschaft für Film und Medien, 2018.

6

"Nothing Is More Enjoyable
Than Love from Afar":
On Werner Schroeter's *The Death
of Maria Malibran* (1970)

> Jimi Hendrix and Janis Joplin, whom I greatly admired,
> died tragically early. Like Jim Morrison of The Doors, Joplin
> belonged to that club of twenty-seven/twenty-eight-year-olds
> who lose their lives upon becoming radiant, mythical idols at
> the peak of their artistic powers. Maria Malibran, who died
> just after turning twenty-eight, was another of them. I had read
> a great deal about the Franco-Spanish bel canto singer, the
> ultimate diva of divas, even greater than my Maria Callas, who
> died just after finishing a unique, challenging, and exhausting
> concert. Everything I tried to depict in my film The Death of
> Maria Malibran arose from my concern with those artists, all of
> whom I so admired.
>
> — Werner Schroeter

Werner Schroeter's *The Death of Maria Malibran* (1972) opens
with blue title cards which we read the following lines from
Heinrich Heine's poem, "Der Asra": "And my clan is that of Asra,
who must die whenever they love." Werner Schroeter's aesthetic
is derived from German Romanticism, with its theme of love

and death from which Wagner borrowed in his most romantic opera, *Tristan und Isolde*. In the film, extreme passion and longing are transformed into ecstatic and transformative experiences through suffering and death. The characters in the sequence of images in the first ten or so minutes of the film convey desires that are not fully realized. Each scene is composed mostly of the close-ups of two female faces or in some scenes, three transgender women, with rarely a male face. In each scene, we see one face drawing closer to the other, in an attempt to kiss the other, overcome by unspeakable longing. As each brief scene comes to a close, the slow movement of the women stops. The figures are posed in a very stylized manner, and the effect of the lightning makes the faces almost appear unearthly, angelic, against a black background, with their lips barely touching, as if in a painting by Giotto di Bondone.

There is an air of melancholy about the expressions on the women's faces; this is furthered by Schroeter's use of Johannes Brahm's "Alto Rhapsody"; near the end of the sequence, the music shifts to the brisk tempo of Ludwig van Beethoven's "Triple Concerto in C" which heightens the dramatic effect. It is during Beethoven's piece that we see Ingrid Caven and Candy Darling in a medium shot. Ingrid Caven's hands move closer and closer, slowly, to Darling's face. Candy is a kind of Baudelarian decadent, with make-up that makes him appear like a damned angel; the extreme lighting lends a sensuous aura to the scene; it is also as if these scenes take place in a remote aesthetic universe apart from reality. As Caven moves her hand closer to Candy's neck, as if in an attempt to kiss him, he turns away from her with a dramatic gesture; we are not sure if she is going to caress him, kiss him, or strangle him. The erotic tension has an element of danger. His tears are a result of his inability to voice his passion; he remains apart in a world of his own. But her tears are *not* the result of her inability to move him emotionally. In love we are trapped in our own subjective reality and cannot really see the other.

In one scene, Magdalena runs through an open field with ships in the distance; she has a gun in her hand; Candy approaches. Magdalena brandishes a gun[1]; Candy is unafraid. The scene has a mock western or even Noir-like quality. Magdalena and Candy, competing divas, are driven by extreme passion towards each other, but their desire is constrained, perhaps by envy. At one point, Candy says "But when you say I love you / my eyes are filled with bitter tears." They fall on top of each other, even after the gun "goes off"; there is no sound except for the up tempo classical piano music on the soundtrack which creates a contrast between the emotion expressed between Candy and Magdalena and the soundtrack. They express their pain and despair as they fall to the ground in an embrace. At one point they both have guns and the scene is repeated with variations. Passion leads to an awkward but ecstatic performance of desire. But even suffering is transformative and in death they consummate their love.

Throughout the film, Schroeter uses various texts drawn from classic literature to create a resonance between the language and the images on the screen. In the scene where Manuela[2] is reading a text from Lautreamont's *Les Chants de Maldoror,* we see Candy Darling next to her listening attentively. Darling's gestures and facial expressions in this scene seemingly run through the entire vocabulary of a silent screen actress conveying a lover in despair or going mad. The text Manuela is reading speaks of a mad woman who "looks back through the mist of her mind" at her "hopes and former happiness...shattered by the turmoil of unarmed powers...her gracefulness is gone, her former beauty." It is as if Candy goes mad upon hearing these words, just as a lover will descend into suffering and potential madness upon learning that the beloved does not return their

---

1   The gun is more a kind of absurd phallic symbol; it is so small; it is like a toy; in another sense, their brandishing of the "tiny gun" is Schroeter's attack on male patriarchy.

2   Schroeter met Manuela Riva, a trans singer, who had a prominent role in the film, in a gay bar in Ludwigshafen.

love. It is the seduction of poetic language i.e. like love letters which drives the lover mad with desire; Candy's exaggerated and histrionic gestures convey this perfectly. If the women in the opening sequence could speak, they might say something like what Manuela reads from *Maldoror*: "the madwoman...is too proud to complain, and will die without revealing her secret to those who are interested in her." The nature of this secret is the source of their overwhelming passion for the other: homosexual desire. The scene concludes with Manuela speaking of a scroll that falls from the bosom of the madwoman; it is found by a young man who reads the text at night in his room alone. Manuela concludes her reading by saying that what follows is the text that the young man in *Les Chants de Maldoror* reads. ... *The Death of Maria Malibran* is essentially a film from the point of view of Lautreamont's woman driven mad by desire.

Schroeter also uses a clip of Sir Laurence Olivier in the role of *Hamlet* reading from act 4, scene 4 of the play, while, simultaneously, we see on the screen Manuela, Candy, Magdalena, and Ingrid, sitting next to each other, elegantly dressed. In the scene from the play, Hamlet is contemplating whether he will enter into the battle against Fortinbras's army; he is wracked by guilt at his inability to choose the right course of action:

> What is a man,
> If his chief good and market of his time
> Be but to sleep and feed? a beast, no more.
> Sure, he that made us with such large discourse,
> Looking before and after, gave us not
> That capability and god-like reason
> To fust in us unused.

He imagines all the men who will die in battle and concludes that to fight is the honorable thing to do:

> Rightly to be great
> Is not to stir without great argument,
> But greatly to find quarrel in a straw

When honour's at the stake. How stand I then,
That have a father kill'd, a mother stain'd,
Excitements of my reason and my blood,
And let all sleep? while, to my shame, I see
The imminent death of twenty thousand men,
That, for a fantasy and trick of fame,
Go to their graves like beds, fight for a plot
Whereon the numbers cannot try the cause,
Which is not tomb enough and continent
To hide the slain? O, from this time forth,
My thoughts be bloody, or be nothing worth!

On the screen, at the point when Olivier utters the words, "a beast….,"[3] we see a blonde-haired man stretched out on the floor, using his arms and feet to move across the left to the right side of the screen. This is the "beast" that must die. When Manuela first sees him, she makes a dramatic gesture of surprise and delight; Candy extends her cupped hand toward his head in a gesture of acceptance and recognition of the young man's beauty. Magdalena slowly assumes a pose, looking up and down at the young man; she is deep in thought. Ingrid moves in a slightly erratic way as if she is troubled by the appearance of the young man. Eventually, the man dies. There is a similar scene is Schroeter's *Neurasia* (1969) where a naked man goes through the same motions, as if crawling with great difficulty across the floor and dies; there, Carla Aulaulu grieves over his dead body. She and the women here, collectively, play out the role of Isolde grieving over Tristan's body in Wagner's opera. The scene is a visual representation of the Liebestod. Candy appears alone in the next scene, shot in black and white, as the following lines from Hamlet are heard:

---

3   The lines from *Hamlet*, "What is a man, / If his chief good and market of his time / Be but to sleep and feed? a beast, no more," would have had a special meaning for Schroeter; Monika Keppler said about Schroeter, that he rejected "any kind of bourgeois life. What he liked best was when someone phoned, and he could say, 'I must pack quickly. I have to go to Paris tomorrow.' He liked to travel and absorb the world."

That, for a fantasy and trick of fame,
Go to their graves like beds, fight for a plot
Whereon the numbers cannot try the cause,
Which is not tomb enough and continent
To hide the slain?

Throughout the reading of these lines, Candy, with her eyes closed, gestures as if she is in despair because of conflicting thoughts, like Hamlet at this moment in the play; her hands (clenched into fists) cover her face as she bends over; then she begins to rise up, covering her face with her hands. At the lines, "O, from this time forth, / My thoughts be bloody, or be nothing worth!", her eyes open and stare directly at the camera. It is a powerful scene. This sequence is an example of Schroeter's use of disjunction between sound and image but also the random synchronization between the lines and the image. I imagine the various reactions of the women as aspects of a single "madwoman," secret diva and muse behind the film; there is surprise, there is affection, there is intellectual curiosity, and there is the inability to act on their desires. Schroeter has written, "Love, a word easy to say / and yet so hard for me."

This disjunction between the images and the sound is Schroeter's form of cinematic anarchism. Monika Keppler writes, "If he described himself as an anarchist, it was never in any concrete political sense. He was an individualist in his anarchism." In program notes, written when he was directing the opera *Wally* in 1985, Schroeter wrote, "Artists and anarchists are united in refusing to submit to what is intolerable in the world as it exists. They have the courage to break the norms of reality." During the "Hamlet sequence," I thought of all the gay men who fought for the right to express themselves over the years, of the Stonewall riots ("my thoughts be bloody, or not at all"), and even of the recent disturbing violence and reactionary anger from conservatives against transgender people. The women's ability to express themselves fully is thwarted; the death of the young man represents the eradication of the male for the transgender woman in her attempt to realize her true self. This "other" must die. Schroeter writes: "But the old myths say, truthfully, that those who see themselves in the mirror as a duality…will die. The myth of Narcissus and his romantic double, who meet in death, has fascinated me since childhood."

In the beginning of the film, we see Magdalena, wearing a long elegant red dress, torn at the side, acting as if in a daze. Behind her, for a brief moment, we see a dead man in the background. The suggestion is that she has been violated by the man and killed him as a result. A similar scene is repeated late in the film, where Malibran and her opera singer friend are curtseying after their anguish over the death of a man.[4] During this scene, we hear "O Mio Babbino Caro," the aria from Puccini's *Gianni Schicchi,* sung by Maria Callas. In the background we see the shadow of the man who has hung himself. Passion and longing are dangerous and the realization of one's true nature can lead to the death of the other in oneself.

I would like to examine a complex sequence in the film that begins in passion and longing and ends in death, which illustrates Schroeter's radical use of images and music over an extended period. Magdalena goes out at night, cruising, and meets a tall blonde man (Darling as a man). She is wide-eyed and innocent, her hands held tight in prayer. In a medium close-up Darling takes hold of one of her hands and turns his head dramatically away from her. In the next scene, partly to the sound of Marty Robbins singing "Carmen Tonight," we see, in an extreme long shot, the same tall blonde man (Darling) walking quickly in a public park and the woman in a suit jacket and skirt (Magdalena) attempting to follow him, but tripping and falling; she cries out as she follows him: "Alfred! Wait for me. Don't leave me. Wait." The dubbing is "bad," since, though the scene is shot from a great distance above, her words seem to have been recorded in a small room. Curiously, the entire effect ends up

---

4   William E. Jones suggests this man may be "Malibran's and her sister, Viardot's dictatorial father, Manuel Garcia." Jones quotes the line from Puccini's *Gianni Schicchi*: "Oh my dear papa, I love him, he is handsome, handsome…." In a sense, all the men who die in the film, can be seen as a reflection of Manuel Garcia.

accentuating the sensation of Magdalena's suffering. Starting from the middle of this scene and going on until the end, we hear Marty Robbins singing the following words from the song "Carmen Tonight," over which we hear Magdalena's cries. As he turns a corner in the park, we hear the following:

> Tonight, I am aching, my body is shaking
> Tonight, Carmen's coming back home
> Tonight, there'll be no room for tears in my bedroom
>
> Tonight, Carmen's coming back home
> Tonight, as I stand here I notice my hand here
> Is trembling as never before

The song concerns a man who has complex feelings as he is returning home to his wife, after not having seen her for a long time; there is a sense of guilt and at times, hatred for his wife. In the next scene, we see Magdalena, leaning on a tree, praying. Her face contorted in expressions of grief and longing as she gazes up at the sky. Finally, she looks down, with an air of dejection. During this scene we hear:

> My feelings I can't hide, resistance has all died
> My pride will rush outside
> The moment she walks through the door
>
> The lips that have kissed her
> That's loved her and missed her

Then Schroeter cuts to a scene of Christine Kaufman, a strikingly beautiful woman, who is smoking a cigarette, and gazing in a coldly seductive way at the camera. During this brief scene we hear the continuation of the verse above (those lips that have kissed her…): "Are lips that have cursed her at night." In the next scene, we see Manuela singing and performing, wearing a glittering long elegant dress, with Kaufman sitting on

the ground next to her moving her body to the rhythm of Manuela's song, while smoking; it is an extension of the previous
scene of Christine in close-up. The song Manuela is performing, as she gestures and tosses her head, is unknown; we only
see her mouth moving as we hear Robbins on the soundtrack
(at one point there is a close up of Manuela tossing her head
and we hear, surprisingly, on the soundtrack: "I'm nervous, I'm
trembling, recalling remembering / The way that she tosses her
head"):

In anguish and torment, I've cursed as the night went
From darkness till dawn's golden light
I thought of just taking these two hands and breaking
The body I'm waiting to touch
I find while I'm waiting, there's no time for hating
While anticipating, the woman I've wanted so much

I've placed pretty flowers to brighten the hours
I put brand new sheets on the bed
I'm nervous, I'm trembling, recalling remembering
The way that she tosses her head

I've given much thought to the fact that I ought to
Have more control over my life
How can I fight it, how can I deny it
There's no way to hide it
The love that I have for my wife

Then there is a moment of silence, but Manuela still continues
to perform. The song is repeated from the beginning and after a few minutes, Schroeter cuts to a scene of Magdalena in a
kind of cage (made of a large screen) with a naked young man
next to her. In the next scene, Magdalena obsessively runs her
fingers through her hair; it is a private gesture which suggests
she is nervous. Often in Schroeter's later films, notably in *Day
of the Idiots*, we enter the private emotional space of a character
where they are often gesturing or doing something obsessively

that seems bizarre relative to the outside world. Magdalena says, "I long for you so much. This means death for me." Presumably, she is talking about the man in the park. Then there is a scene that shows a complex arrangement of three bodies in the cage; Magdalena to the left of the cage and on the right two naked men facing each other; she holds onto one of the men's arms. She concludes about Alfred, "I should have not given him my love!" Finally, we realize he is dead.

The effect of this complex sequence in terms of the song and the images on the screen, is that alternative and shifting realities occur simultaneously: there is the man in the song who is almost afraid of returning to his wife; an image of Alfred walking away from Magdalena; and the scenes in the cage, where the viewer enters Magdalena's private space, where she speaks about the man in her life and where we are told that he is dead (in keeping with the Romantic theme of love and its relation to death). The film moves from the outside world of the park to the private space of the woman, Magdalena, which is in conflict with reality. The music does not complement the images in the way film music usually does, by aligning with the images and highlighting and enforcing the emotional tone. Instead, in Schroeter's montage, the image and the song generate a space between them that allows a viewer to create alternative readings. The "Hamlet scene" uses the excessive gestures of the women upon seeing the young man to create a kind of irrational sequence, more akin to dreams, which opens up a space in the viewer's mind where reason yields to thought that is associative; it is the mode from which poetry arises. As a viewer we are asked to interpret multiple realities that occur simultaneously and to see, or rather, feel, resonances, in the spaces in between the image and the sound. I have not mentioned all the opera excerpts that were played after Robbin's song in the sequence, since I wanted to focus on the relation between the words of that song and the images; it also shows Schroeter's creative use of a pop song. Indeed, one could spend many hours searching out the references in a Schroeter film. In *The Death of Maria Malibran,* he creates a complex montage that opens up the possibility of numerous interpretations around a single theme: death and its relation to love.

Schoeter also uses silence in relation to sound for dramatic effect in the film. At times, the dramatic music will abruptly stop while the character is in the midst of expressing an extreme emotion that will continue in silence. There is a scene where Christine Kaufman, as Malibran's father, holds a knife to her throat; she screams but there is no sound at all. The effect is unsettling and powerful and evocative of the silent era in film. We saw this use of silence previously in the "Hamlet" sequence where Candy was alone. Scenes such as these draw the viewer's attention to the materiality of the image; abstract sound exists in a space apart from the material image. This opens an alternate space between the sound a viewer is hearing in its relation to the absence of sound and the image he is watching. This is not intellectual like in a Godard film such as *2 or 3 Things I Know about Her,* where he manipulates the soundtrack to draw attention to the way sound manipulates a viewer's emotions, but somatic; this is Schroeter's romantic sensibility.

This lack of correspondence between sound/image also mirrors the character's inability to voice their desire, trapped as they are in a world of the imagination. The lover hears something that may not correspond to what he is seeing; alternately, the emotion felt (expressed in the music of the film) may not correspond exactly to what is seen on the screen. In this way, Schroeter destabilizes our sense of hierarchies, and the dominance of rational thought. Passion is not rational. In Schroeter's films, lovers give themselves over to the beloved, almost selflessly, but are often unable to fully realize their desire or are rejected. This sets up the condition where passion faces either death or love. Schroeter writes, "The unconditionality of emotion is anything but foolishness, for unconditionality already means two possibilities: death and love."

There are two concepts of love in European culture, one that derives from the Greeks and another that derives from a different strain in the Middle Ages and the Renaissance which influenced German romantic ideas of love and its relation to death.

For the Greeks, love was harmonious, and it was thought that through this deeper understanding such harmony and well-being was achieved. The Greeks regarded passion as a burden that would lead to melancholy. For Wagner, nothing was sweeter than love-death. Thomas Mann would write in a notebook, "To long for love to the verge of dying for it, and yet to despise everyone who loves. Happiness is not in being loved; it is satisfaction mixed with disgust for vanity. Happiness is loving and not making even the tiniest approach towards the object of one's love." This yearning, unfulfilled aspect of love is a product of the Middle Ages: Jaufre Rudel, the 12th-century troubadour, wrote: "Nothing is more enjoyable than love from afar."

Schroeter said of the film that it was about "love, the death of the beloved, and lamentation for the dead — inspired by the cult of the diva." The diva referred to in the title of film is the 19th-century opera singer Maria Malibran, who was a legend in her time. Rossini wrote of her: "Ah! That wonderful creature! With her disconcerting musical genius she surpassed all who sought to emulate her, and with her superior mind, her breadth of knowledge and unimaginable fieriness of temperament she outshone all other women I have known..." One of her earliest biographers, Ernest Legouvé, described her singing voice as "golden"; Malibran's vocal range was incredibly wide, ranging from E♭ below middle C to high C and D, which allowed her to effortlessly sing roles designed for a contralto as well as a high soprano. It was her performances of Bellini, Rossini, and Donizetti that led to their popularity in the US and Europe.

She was born in Paris to a famous Spanish musical family as María Felicitas García Sitches. Her father, Manuel García, a famous tenor greatly admired by Rossini, had created the role of Count Almaviva in his *The Barber of Seville.* García was also a composer of note and an influential vocal instructor; he was Maria's first vocal coach. He was described as inflexible and tyrannical; as a result, he was often in conflict with his daughter who had an ego as powerful as his own. She was known for her stormy personality and intense way of life. In the film, Candy Darling plays a young girl dominated by her mother, which invokes the relationship Malibran had with her father. There is also a wonderfully absurd sequence where a diva in the film sings an aria off key; it is indeed a "terrible" performance. Candy who accompanies her on the piano is visibly shocked and embarrassed for her. Schroeter is not above having some fun with the idea of the diva. These "bad" performances that occur in Schroeter's films are a way of his attacking the idea of a perfect performance and drawing attention to intensity and desire, which, in this film, does not achieve its goal. Malibran rose to enormous heights in the world of opera but through a kind of freak accident where she fell off a horse, the seriousness of which she ignored, she later died after a recital; she was only twenty-eight old. For Schroeter, her death, "set the seal on the tragic intensity with which she lived, and that attracted me because it is a strong theme in my work."

Another diva, the trans actress and model, Candy Darling, also died at the young age of 29 years old after living an intense life as one of Andy Warhol's entourage. Schroeter met her in New York during a visit there with Magdalena in 1971. Schroeter wrote about meeting her:

Candy was a slim, tall, very blonde creature with a delicately shimmering, porcelain-like face. She took huge quantities of hormone tablets in order to rid herself of her other, earlier identity as James Lawrence Slattery from Brooklyn. With Warhol's help, she aimed to turn herself into a movie-star love goddess in the mold of Jean Harlow, Marilyn Monroe, and Rita Hayworth...I admired her elegance, her beauty, and her melancholy, all the result of the radical way she was changing her body, working on it as you might on a work of art. Candy's health was wrecked by the hormone treatments; she died at the age of just twenty-nine, only three years after we were all working together...Candy's radical self-transformation fascinated me; it was a truly pioneering act in that repressive period.

Malibran served as the model for Schroeter's divas, which included the one most important to him, Maria Callas. I would also include Anita Cerquetti, another great bel canto diva, whom Schroeter greatly admired. Cerquetti lost "her divine voice" while young and quit singing at the height of her fame; she was twenty-five years old at the time. But what she shared with Callas and all the other great divas, as well as Malibran herself, is the ability, "to live out the few basic moments of human expression to musical and gestural excess — to convey in their totality and without psychological analysis these few completely tenable emotions: life, love, happiness, hate, jealousy and mortal fear."

The women in *The Death of Maria Malibran* suffer because they are unable to fully realize their desires or are rejected by homosexual men. Schroeter identified more with the women in his films and, particularly, with the transgender women Manuela Riva and Candy Darling. In the film, Schroeter is obsessed with death and its connection to love and the idea that self-realization is also linked with the death of the male: the desire of the transgender man to fully embody herself. But love is the problem. The following excerpt from László F. Földényi's book, *Melancholy,* perfectly captures the essence of Schroeter's film:

> When one falls in love, one has been seduced; one falls in love with the other person with such force, losing oneself and one's place in the customary scheme of things to such an extent, that a doubt inevitably arises whether it is a matter of seduction. The object of love seduces the lover, even if the "object" knows nothing about what he or she has provoked. Just as a lover does not choose his object of love, that person is chosen through "the machinations of hell," (Kleist, *Werke und Briefe,* 2:26), so the object of love is seductive in a deeper sense...the lover, who has been seduced, enjoys the plunge into love, by which he hastens from himself into the other.

Of all of Schroeter's films, *The Death of Maria Malibran* is the most explicit film on this experience of love-death, which evokes the Liebestod of Wagner's opera, and most clearly places him in a visionary German Romantic tradition.

Works Cited

Földényi, László F. *Melancholy*. New Haven: Yale University Press, 2016.

Schroeter, Werner. Booklet included in *Eika Katappa* (1969) & *Der Tod de Maria Malibran* (1972), dir. Werner Schroeter. Filmmuseum Munich, 2014. DVD.

Schroeter, Werner, and Claudia Lenssen. *Days of Twilight, Nights of Frenzy*. Translated by Anthea Bell. Chicago: University of Chicago Press, 2017.

7

The Conflict between Love and Passion: On Werner Schroeter's *Willow Springs* (1972)

In *Willow Springs* (1972), Schroeter exposes the conflict between passion and love by exploring the inner desires and conflicts among three women, Magdalena, Ila, and Christine, through the characters' spatial orientation, their poses and theatrical gestures, and various kinds of music, ranging from opera to pop. Interestingly, Magdalena (Montezuma), Ila (von Hasperg), and Christine (Kaufman) are the names of the actresses and they were all close friends of Schroeter's. The film was shot in a remote setting in the Mojave Desert.

Schroeter wrote the script and Magdalena also contributed a great deal to it as well as being responsible for the clothes and make-up. Christine N. Brinchmann writes, "They stayed in Los Angeles for a while, taking drugs, developing ideas, creating characters and storylines together, collecting costumes for the film-to-be, and driving around location-hunting…the film represents…a document of the (musical and other) tastes of the group at the time, their dreams and images of themselves, and their desire for role-playing." About their experience, Schroeter writes:

Willow Springs is the reflection of the situation we were living and that I had felt while working for several years with
the three women, Magdalena, Ila, and Christine. In a poetic
way, Ila put her ugliness up front, Christine was coldly beautiful and very friendly, and the third Magdalena, very depressive and dominant. The situation had been created in a
very unfavorable political space, with fascists all around. The
town was run by an American Nazi. A really scary place…In
the end we found ourselves in the same situation as the protagonists of the film. We were in a little hotel six miles from
Willow Springs and completely cut off."

Schroeter suggests an intersection between politics and the
personal lives of the women and Daniel in the resulting film.
For example, their experience with "the fascist" was transposed
onto the character Magdelana plays, who plays a domineering
woman in the film, a kind of "fascist." About Christine Kaufman, who played the "cool aesthete" in the film, Schroeter
writes that she was "a former child star bullied by her mother,"
who wasn't interested in acting on the stage when he casted her
in a production of Lessing's *Emilia Galotti* right after the filming
of *Willow Springs*. She had also appeared in his previous film,
The Death of Maria Malibran (1972). In *Willow Springs,* her parents are dead. The barbie doll that she holds in the film suggests
her lost youth as a child star. In the film she says, "I have never
loved anyone but the child that died inside of me before it was
born." Ila von Hapsburg, who had been editing Schroeter's films
since *Salome* (1972), was suffering from a painful inflammation
and also a dental abcess. They had almost no money and did
not know what to do. In his biography, Schroeter writes of going
to Las Vegas and marrying Jutta, "the girlfriend of my youth.[1]

---

1   Two years later they divorced in Germany. About the time, Schroeter
    writes, "Jutta had petitioned for the divorce; we had never lived in the
    same place, and directly after the wedding I had returned to Los Angeles,
    moving on later to Munich and elsewhere, while Jutta went on traveling
    in her job as an air hostess. Being the free spirits that we were, we went
    to the divorce court together hand in hand. Or maybe I wasn't there for

She came from Oberflockenbach in the Bergstrasse district. She could help us out financially. Magdalena, not surprisingly, reacted in a very dominant and depressive way." Magdalena Montezuma would go on to appear in Schroeter's films until the end of her life and he considered her his muse; she was a brilliant performer in many of his films. Michael O'Daniels played the man in the film. He allowed Schroeter to use parts from his actual diary. About him, Schroeter writes, "He had been introduced to me by acquaintances in Los Angeles. I thought him erotically very attractive and spent a good deal of time with him. He was an American beauty from the southern states, a dreamer who drifted when he had been taking drugs." In the film, in order to escape from his bourgeois background, he decides to travel, and ends up at the women's house. The real life tensions, conflicts, and erotic situations resonate with those in the film: Christine, a child star, is cold and distant and lives in her world of music and beauty; Magdalena, the "fascist," is domineering and aggressive in asserting control over the two women; Ila, the least attractive of the women, is shy and withdrawn, and suffers because of her love for Daniel. Daniel is travelling in the film, as he did in real life, and trying to escape his earlier life and his mother. Schroeter is not only the director of the film but also a participant in the lives of the women; he, like Ila in the film, was attracted to Daniel in real life. In this way, the separation between Art and Life collapsed when making the film.

Early in the film, Magdalena delivers a speech which has all the qualities of something you might hear a cult leader say or a Nazi, for that matter. She begins her speech: "Oh my companions, preserve the purity of your hands / that deny lascivious temptation." She continues:

> You possess the purity of those who spill the blood of others…you will never be afraid again. I am the force who led you here…I love you more than I love myself…I take away

---

the proceedings at all? The grounds for divorce were that we hadn't had marital intercourse since November 1972, which was obvious."

your fear and your hope. I do not want to know where you are or what you are. I want to consider your actions. I am the fulfillment. I am the force through which we live.

At this point Ila and Christine, kneeling to the right and left of Magdalena who stands over them, as if she is the high priestess at a Black Mass, repeat her words. They also repeat the final words of Magdalena's speech, addressing her: "She is the force through which we breathe." The whole scene is dark except for a row of lit candles on an improvised altar, which we later find out is a bar. This is testament to Schroeter's resourcefulness in making the film; the film was made with a minimal budget and a small crew. Magdalena speaks of "purity" and "blood" invoking the Nazi obsession with a pure Aryan strain. She is not concerned with Ila and Christine as individuals, with their own needs and desires; she is only interested in their actions and how they can serve her. And like any cult leader, she envisions herself as a kind of god at the beginning of the film: "I am the fulfillment." Magdalena is able to enforce an ironclad hold on the women by putting Ila and Christine under a kind of spell and using a kind of mystical language. Schroeter described her character in the film as a "kind of saint and wise woman, a lesbian and a pow-erful character." Without any psychological attempt to define the personality of the characters in the film, through character development, their identities remain fluid. Magdalena is both a fascist and a saint. Indirectly, this may also be an attack on the Catholic Church.

In a key scene, Schroeter uses the camera to create a unified locus that creates a visual, subliminal bond between two char-acters. The sequence begins with Christine on her bed listening to various opera records and combing her hair. She only listens to a few minutes of a record before playing a different record and appears deep in thought. From the open door to her room, Magdelana watches her, with an expression of longing on her face. Magdelana, with her stylized hand gestures, and subtle fa-cial expressions, gives voice to an entire range of emotions mod-ulating between longing and despair. Suddenly, in an instant,

Christine turns towards the camera; she is looking directly at Magdalena but also at the audience; thus, the audience is also looking at Christine from the point of view of Magdalena. The camera is the locus through which they gaze at each other for a brief moment. In another scene, Christine is standing next to a window, in a dream-state; Magdalena, outside, approaches the window, her face slightly out of focus. She gazes at Christine who is unaware of her presence; she looks at her from a position above her, thus asserting her dominance, until we see her in close-up. Private space in the film is continually being invaded by the gaze of someone from the outside.

About halfway through the film, we see Daniel in his room, apparently deep in thought, gazing outside the window, and on the soundtrack, we hear him reading from his journal. It is a lavishly decorated room, worthy of something out of a Luchino Visconti film. The young man is of a bourgeoise class. On the soundtrack, we hear the line: "life is a thing of tears and smiles." He seems tormented. He relates a story of his mother going out and getting drunk. There is a close up of a photo of a man in military uniform. Is this his father? Did he fight in the war on the side of the Germans? Is he dead? If he is, then Daniel is alone with a dominant, alcoholic mother, a recipe for disaster. About his own mother, Schroeter wrote: "My mother was a lovable and indeed a loving woman, although she had her flaws, like every other human being. She clung to the love of her sons, which was sometimes difficult for my brother, who never entirely managed to break away from my parents." At a point in the film, Daniel's mother visits the women's home. They are suspicious of this stranger. When Daniel appears and see his mother, he just looks at her without saying a word; his mother turns away from him, with a sudden realization that she is no longer welcome at the house. What has she realized about her son that should make her suddenly leave him alone? In real life, his mother could have been angry about his drug use, or his homosexuality. But in the film, the scene sheds no light on the relationship between mother and son except that we get the indication that she felt her son should be left alone to pursue his own life.

At one point, Daniel gazes out of the window in his room and Schroeter then cuts to a scene where someone else is looking out of a window; it is Christine gazing at Daniel who has just emerged from a cab that pulled up in front of the house the women share. The field of Christine and Daniel's vision is linked by the cut which creates a bond between them. The cut also creates a link between Daniel in the past and in the present. Christine begins to talk to Daniel.[2] But we see, on the floor above, that Magdalena is also looking at the new arrival. Both of the women are looking at the same man; this creates a visual triangle, whose apex is Daniel, and suggests that he is the center of their conflict with each other. Windows are important for Schroeter and appear in many of his films. They suggest escape, or hope, but such hope remains futile and escape simply a dream. Ila is immediately attracted to Daniel and more his "type." The suggestion in the film is that she is from the working class and so her connection to Magdalena and Christine is as someone who is exploited; she is not a dreamer but a realist and a sexual adventurer.

In the "water fetching" scene and in the scene at the bar, Schroeter uses the orientation of the characters to express the conflict and desire between them. In the "water fetching" scene, Christine, wearing her elegant red dress, is seen from a distance, standing in front of a door on the upper level of the house; Ila is on the ground level, standing to the far right of Christine; she is

---

2   In a later conversation, Christine tells Daniel that she prefers "to surrender responsibility for my life to Magdalena because she loves pain and the beauty of her face is the beauty of pain." Daniel tells her that he grew up in Hawaii, in a house on the beach, and led a nomadic life, travelling to the Orient and countries in Europe; he led a kind of privileged life. He tells her, "I really like the city, but I like the country more." His decision to hitchhike across America has led him to the women's home. The young man speaks in English and Christine in German, but they describe very different experiences. Christine is at home in her dream world, secluded in this house. Her parents are dead. But Daniel desires to escape his bourgeois confinement and see the world. Daniel can relate to much of what Christine says even though they fail to finally understand each other since; the main reason for this is that he wants to travel and live life, but she is content to stay in the house.

asked to fetch water from the well; she moves forward, toward the well, in the foreground; as she does, Magdalena appears, behind her, standing where Ila was previously, in the doorway on the ground level. Ila dominates the screen, from her position in the foreground; a visual triangle is formed by Magdalena, Christine, and Ila which suggests their relations: Ila is in the foreground; Christine is on an upper level of the house, but appears smaller, because of the distance; Magdalena assumes the position formerly held by Ila on the ground floor but also appears smaller in the distance like Christine; this suggests they are the same in their relation to Ila, who is the apex of the triangle; they both have a problem with Ila because she is in love with Daniel. Schroeter creates a dynamic geometric space that suggests the conflict, without using language or examining the psychology of the characters. The manner in which Schroeter frames the entire scene also evokes a scene in an opera. It is artificial and staged.

In the scene at the bar, Christine, Ila, Magdalena, and Daniel are seen in closeup and posed. On each face is a different expression: Christine, standing behind the bar, is looking into the distance; Magdalena is looking at her, also behind the bar; Ila and Daniel are gazing at each other in front of the bar. No one is moving. It is a tableau, where each character reflects on his position in relation to the other and the importance of the gaze is central. Schroeter manipulates the compositional elements of a scene to create a sense of sophisticated elegance. His positioning of the bodies suggests emotional tension and heighten the drama as in a painting or an opera.

Other scenes seem to exist outside the present time of the film and are dream-like; in the film we cannot be sure which scenes are dreams, reality, or hallucinations. In one of these scenes, we see Christine and Magdalena in the desert, both wearing glittering black robes. Christine is seen with her red fan open, covering her face in profile; as she closes the fan, she gazes in the distance and sees Magdalena walking towards her; Christine puts out her hand in a gesture of acceptance. When Magdalena is face to face with Christine, Christine raises her left hand; Magdalena mirrors her movement with her right hand,

and they touch each other's palms. She gazes at Christine. But Christine looks off into the distance and not at Magdalena. We are not fully given the reasons behind their actions; they are suggestive more than defined. The scene does not relate to the past or the future; it exists in a kind of timeless present. They use mysterious gestures that suggest silent communion. Wolf Wondratschek, speaking about the characters in Schroeter's films, has said that they "act according to a riddle for which, as of now, there is no certain meaning."[3]

Schroeter's unique framing of the stylized and theatrical gestures of the women evoke the world of opera, a world Schroeter knew well[4], and achieve subtle modulations of emotion, creating tension and high drama. In the scene where Magdalena rips the doll and red fan from Christine, they both move with intense and theatrical gestures, with opera on the soundtrack, that creates an effect of high drama. Helped by Christine's elegant red dress, the overall effect of the scene is a soprano in jeopardy. We almost expect her to launch into an aria, as she attempts to escape by scaling the wall. But it is a useless gesture. She is trapped.

There is another scene, where Magdalena is standing next to a gas pump and tells Daniel that there is no gas, suggesting that he has a reason to stay at the house. Magdalena stands at the pump, her body in a styled pose and dressed in black, all of which suggests her sinister intention; and soon after, as she follows Daniel, she not so much walks but slithers behind him as they move toward the house. The poses and hand gestures have a major effect on these scenes. Few words are spoken and there is no development of the psychology of the characters to fully

---

3   This except is from Wolf Wondratschek's talk on Werner Schroeter's films as part of a tribute to Werner Schroeter at the *Biennale* on October 24, 2008. A recording can be found in Werner Schroeter, dir., *Willow Springs & Tag der Idioten* (Filmmuseum München, 2013), DVD.

4   During the late 1980s Schroeter became well known in Europe and abroad for his many theater and opera productions, winning many awards. His documentary on opera and opera singers, *Poussières d'amour,* was released in 1996.

explain their actions. This causes the audience not to feel any-thing for the characters, as in a typical Hollywood film, where there is character development, even when Magdalena murders them.

At one point in the film, the sequence of events is reversed; effect precedes cause. This involves Magdalena's murder of Dan-iel and the women. Magdalena has a dream of shooting Chris-tine and Daniel as they try to escape. This actually happens as they try to escape near the end of the film. This stylistic effect is common in Schroeter's films. The film, "is a work more of performance than story, more of texture, color, music, and ges-ture than of rigorous structure. It holds the spectator in what Michelle Langford calls 'haptic fascination,' addressing us not so much intellectually as somatically." Eventually, Magdalena kills both the lovers as well as Christine, and walks away, wearing her black robe, and fades into the distance. About this ending, Schroeter wrote, "And Christine too, awoken by the shots [both Ila and Daniel are dead at this point], stands in the doorway, failing to understand the situation as she greets her dehuman-ized mistress, and she too, is mowed down by gunshots. Mag-dalena disappears into the desert, not knowing *to this day* [my emphasis] where she made her mistake." Schroeter speaks of the film as though it is an event from real-life, perhaps alluding to Magdalena's reaction to his brief marriage to Jutta or the women and Daniel.

Magdalena is perhaps the most complex figure in the film. She has experienced suffering in the beginning of the film she is raped by a biker. As a result, she struggles to express her emo-tions. On the surface she dominates Christine, but, in a sense, Christine is made for her, and stronger than her, colder, in fact, as she lives in a fantasy world of music and beauty that distanc-es her from Magdalena. About her character, Schroeter wrote, "Christine loves music and has a tenuous relationship to reality." In another sense, she represents the dangers of being an artist, dangers that Schroeter himself must have been aware of. In a later film, *Day of the Idiots* (1981), the main female character, played by Carole Bouquet, repeats the phrase "I don't want to dream…I want to live." For Schroeter, the ideal way of living was with just "two or three suitcases, a good hotel, maybe a crate of books and music as well."

In his films, Schroeter uses various kinds of music to under-score or comment on a scene, as well as serve as ironic counter-point. In *Willow Springs* he uses music as a leitmotiv. In the scene where Christine and Daniel talk for the first time, we hear clas-sical music while Christine is speaking, and rough country-like music while Daniel is speaking; Daniel is a country boy at heart. The country music is so loud on the soundtrack it threatens to drown out Daniels words.[5] The different music underscores the difference between them. Daniel has more in common with Ila, whose leitmotiv is the Andrews Sisters hit from 1944, "Rum and Coca Cola," which is about a mother and daughter in Trinidad working as prostitutes for American soldiers. The song's sugges-tion of sex for pay is appropriate for the relation between Ila, a working woman and sexual adventurer, and Daniel, a bourgeois young man. But love, in many ways, is always a transaction and finally, it is their love for each other that leads to the tragedy at the end of the film. In conversation with Foucault about the dif-ference between love and passion, Schroeter says that "passion contains in itself a great communicative force, whereas love is an isolated state. I find it very depressing to know that love is a creation and interior invention."[6]

---

5   These instances of "bad" dubbing will occur in Schroeter's early films where they suggest his indifference to the idea of perfection; it also an attack on the use of music in a typical Hollywood film, where such "mis-takes" would not be tolerated. For Schroeter, emotion dictates the choices in his films rather than adherence to an established practice.

6   Foucault largely agrees with Schroeter's idea that "love is less active than passion." When Schroeter asks Foucault whether he has a greater "tenden-cy for passion or love," Foucault responds that passion is more important to him, though passion can "take a turn toward love." But for Schroeter, "love is a lost force, a force that must lose itself immediately because it is never reciprocal. It is always suffering, total nihilism, like life and death." For Schroeter, there were "so few possibilities for communication in life that it was necessary to profit from work to express oneself," to express oneself creatively. This idea of the difference between love and passion is a major theme in Schroeter's films.

The creation of *Willow Springs* happened under unique circumstances. In order to cope with the debts that Schroeter had incurred with his previous film, *The Death of Maria Malibran* (1972), he accepted a project that required him to make a collage film on Andy Warhol, to be titled *The Dream of Marilyn Monroe*, for the German television network ZDF. He received some funding and travelled to Los Angeles. But when he arrived, he lost interest in the project and made *Willow Springs* instead. The network was shocked when they learned that he had made the film, but they eventually accepted the replacement. It's impossible to imagine something that like that happening today. All that remains of the original project is a poster of Marilyn Monroe on the door of Christine's room.

Thinking of Schroeter's style, I am reminded of Giorgio Vasari's comments on the Italian painter Parmigianino's "Self-Portrait in a Convex Mirror" (1523–24):

> In order to investigate the subtleties of art, he set himself one day to make his own portrait, looking at himself in a convex barber's mirror. And in doing this, perceiving the bizarre effects produced by the roundness of the mirror, which twists the beams of a ceiling into strange curves, and makes the doors and other parts of the buildings recede in an extraordinary manner, the idea came to him to amuse himself by counterfeiting everything.[7]

Willow Springs is Schroeter's portrait of himself, as if through the "convex mirror" of his medium, of his passions and despair, as seen in the three women. In his biography, Schroeter writes: "Although my films take life from the evidence of the image in them, never from logical narrative and symbolism, they do disclose inner experience…If desire does not get between me and the other person, then the women, the actress who is my friend,

---

7 Cited in Jonathan Jones, "Self-Portrait in a Convex Mirror (c. 1523–24), Parmigianino," *The Guardian,* January 17, 2003, https://www.theguardian.com/culture/2003/jan/18/art.

is a better surface on which to project the eternal and insupera-
ble conflict between love and passion." *Willow Springs* was made
because Schroeter was driven to examine certain conflicts that
play out in relationships, a subject close to him, instead of what
the German television station told him to do. The inner need
was greater and so the result was one of his best films, and one
of the most important films to come out of the New German
Cinema. The film was awarded the Grand Prix of the Hyères
festival in 1973.

Works Cited

Brinckmann, Christine N. "'Leaping and Lingering': Narrative
    Structure in Werner Schroeter's *Willow Springs* (1973)." In
    Werner Schroeter, edited by Roy Grudmann, 92–105. Vienna:
    Österreichisches Filmmuseum; Synema-Gesellschaft für
    Film und Medien, 2018.
Schroeter, Werner, and Claudia Lenssen. *Days of Twilight,
    Nights of Frenzy.* Translated by Anthea Bell. Chicago:
    University of Chicago Press, 2017.

8

A Neapolitan Family Saga: On Werner Schroeter's *The Kingdom of Naples* (1978)

Like the entire communal life of the city of Naples, the personal development of its individual inhabitants has been unable to withstand the constant, violent infiltration by foreign powers, consumer interests, and tourists. Present-day Naples presents a picture of desperate dissolution, a phenomenon inimical to life and even worse than the social decline of such a Latin American metropolis as Mexico City. The criminal form of anarchy that has taken hold in southern Italy prefigures the development of the whole European continent.

— Werner Schroeter, at the time of the filming of
The Kingdom of Naples

In Werner Schroeter's 1978 Neapolitan family saga, *The Kingdom of Naples* (*Nel Regno Di Napoli*), the Pagano family attempt to carve out a life during the post-war years. Two siblings named Vittoria and Massimo, the father Roberto, and the mother (not named in the film) struggle to avoid economic and sexual exploitation from both capitalists and communists. The Pagano family are surrounded by a cast of characters whose lives intersect with theirs. These characters include a French prostitute, whose name is Rosario à France, called "Frenchie" by her clients, who serves as the midwife at Vittoria's birth; the Pagano's neighbor, Caviola, who prostitutes her young daughter, Rosa, for bags of wheat from America; and the factory owner Puppeta Ferrante (played wonderfully by the great diva, Ida Di Benedetto), who employs Vittoria to clean her apartment, while grooming her to eventually service her male relatives and business friends. In their own way, each character is unable to avoid succumbing to economic forces beyond their control, as they discover they need to potentially prostitute themselves, either for payment or in support of one political agenda or another, in order to survive.

Caviola allows an American GI to have sex with her young daughter and later in the film also tries to marry her off to the wealthy attorney Palumbo who is a homosexual and who supported the Christian Democrats in the post-war years. She does so because she realizes that the husband she married, comrade Simonetti, is unable to provide for her and her daughter. Mrs. Ferrante, a factory owner, attempts to sexually exploit Vittoria to obtain money for her failing enterprise. Sexual and economic exploitation runs rampant in the post-war years. Even Massimo falls in love with the French prostitute who cannot love him in return. Only Vittoria emerges from the wreckage of the post-war years with a job and a taste for languages, which she says she senses will be important in the future. When her ailing father asks her why she doesn't have a husband and instead spends so much time reading books, she responds that she earns enough money to support herself and does not need a man.

While this film shows Schroeter moving away from more experimental style and embracing realism, it is not strictly a realist film, rather, it is structured more like a play with 16 acts, made up of a series of vignettes. While it is certainly more linear than his previous films, it is no less theatrical and dramatic; the entire scene of Caviola's grief over her daughter's death reaches operatic heights of intensity. Rosa's languid movements on her death bed and the mother's grief are is highly dramatic and stylized. Rosa lays in her white nightgown, her mouth open, unable to express her pain at dying. The mother laughs and wails in a fit of madness brought on by intense despair, placing her head on her daughter's dead body. A sudden painful moment of recognition at her failure as a mother comes when she suddenly stops herself from slapping her daughter's face as she lies dead. She is overcome with feelings of rage and despair at her death and also her failure as a mother to save her.

A similar dramatic effect occurs during the scene of Roberto's wife's death; her body wracked with pain and she convulses on the bed. As she pulls her bed covers aside, we see that her white nightgown is stained with blood in the groin area. We also see that she holds tightly onto a cross. While these death scenes are realistic in one sense, they are also slightly overblown, highly dramatic, and give a viewer the sense of the theatre that real life actually is.

After Roberto's wife's death, Schroeter's next sequence of images function poetically and symbolically in a non-linear fashion by using associative rather than rational connections. There is an image of the sky with the camera moving closer to the blue; then a military drumbeat begins, which foreshadows the drumbeat at the carnival scene at the end of the film and extends for the length of the sequence; then the husband screams; then there is an image of Christ; then a shot of the husband in despair; he moves toward the open window where there is a view of the sea; then there is a shot of a large baroque hearse moving through the streets. The use of religious imagery highlights the dominance of the Church in Rome upon the lives of Italians. The window, which is a common feature in Schroeter's films, offers a view of the sea, and signifies an escape from pain, the start of a new life, which is never possible. For a Catholic, the images of Christ and the Virgin Mary hold a certain power over the imagination, especially during the hour of death. Schroeter focuses his camera on an empty sky; is it just that, an empty, yet beautiful sky, or simply a veil behind which there is possibly a transcendent God. As suggested, such Catholic faith is what helps Vittoria avoid being take advantage of by Mrs. Ferrante's customers. Though we must remember that the small figure-head of President Kennedy, which Vittoria brought home one day, along with a poster of him, seems to trump the small religious tokens on the table next to the figure. Money, capitalism, takes the place of the spiritual out of necessity.

The first scene of the film is of a little girl holding a stick on the end of which there is a crumpled piece of paper, as she walks through an empty room, towards an open window; we find out later that this is Vittoria as a child; she leans the improvised white flag out the window, and slowly waves it as a sign of peace. Vittoria is the strongest in her family. Signs of this occur in the scenes when Vittoria and Massimo are children. In one scene, she urges Massimo to wash his face and helps him rub his face with a rag; then she helps him put on his shoes; she loves her brother and wants to take care of him. As they grow, this sibling affection continues. In another scene, Massimo joins the Communist party and Vittoria visits him at the Communist headquarters. She sees him cleaning the floor with a broom and teases him by saying that this is not man's work and that the Communist party is turning him into a wife. He responds by sweeping the dust at her; they tease each other until they break out in laughter and embrace each other, making silly faces in the private language of siblings.

Massimo is told by his communist friends that Kennedy is a colonialist and an imperialist; this idea influences Massimo who previously thought Kennedy was a friend to Italy; but Vittoria disagrees with him and hangs a poster of Kennedy in the house. She also brings home a small figure of Kennedy's face which she places on a table next to her religious tokens. This is the beginning of the split between brother and sister, as he continues to have faith in the Communist party, and she goes the way of Capitol; her study of languages anticipates future globalization. Vittoria believes in America, in the way of capitalism. The same man who was aggressive with her in Mrs. Ferrante's apartment, visits her again in the hotel where she works; she recognizes him and slaps his face. She is a grown woman now and will not tolerate the aggressive actions of men. Indeed, for her, education is important, and she is a realist; she is the image of her mother. Massimo, on the other hand, is a communist and a dreamer and is the image his father, a shoemaker; he will eventually be arrested during a protest and spend two years in prison.

There is a scene in the prison courtyard where Massimo sits apart from the prisoners and daydreams; in the dream sequence that follows, he is seen running on a mountain with scattered snow on the ground and calling out: "Father, Father." We see his father in another part of the mountain struggling to approach him. We are not sure whether he sees Massimo or just hears him. Massimo seeks the love or approval of his father; in a scene, early in the film, Massimo, as a child, and his father are eating dinner; his father demands that he go to school and receive an education. Before Massimo's mother died, his father thought the opposite. In fact, it was the mother who wanted the children to receive an education and the parents fought about it. Regardless of his parents' wishes, Massimo does not want to go to school but earn money instead; and so he joins the Communist party. In real time, the prison guard notices Massimo sitting alone and daydreaming and becomes suspicious of him; he orders him to get up and go among the other prisoners. His father is not a devoted Communist and he is less and less involved with the party as the years pass. He ends his days, alone, so weakened, he can hardly bring the hammer down on the nail in repairing a shoe. The son repeats the failures of the father; it is that way among the poor when life offers no way out.

Massimo started working for the communists as a young boy who believed in their politics, though he, as well as his sister, see no evidence that the living situation in Italy has improved over time. But Massimo is a dreamer, who believed in a "collective conscience" and that the workers will win against the greedy capitalists and that the lives of Italians will improve. He lacks a solid purpose in life. He works for the Communists, for little or no pay, speaks of the "capitalist pigs" and the exploitation of the workers; but the communists act in the same way as the capitalists. When they finally offer him a "real" job, it involves heavy physical work lifting lumber and metal from a pile and loading it onto a truck. At the time, the left-wing press protested the film because Schroeter showed that the Communists were out to enrich themselves in a way no different from the capitalists. Schroeter is not a political filmmaker; he points out problems when they exist, but he shows no devotion to any political ideology; if anything, Schroeter is closer to an anarchist.

In the post-war years, the Christian Democrats were considered largely responsible for the rise in power of the bourgeoisie class in Italian society and the dominance of the Church on people's lives. In the film, we see that the attorney Palumbo rises in society because of his association with the ruling Christian Democrats. There is also a scene in church, early in the film, where the priest loudly denounces the communists as atheists. In 1969, the PCI (Italian Communist Party) was criticized and superseded by the student movement. The final break between the student movement and the PCI occurred during the "Historical Compromise," an alliance between the PCI and the Christian Democrats, the result of which was the people's subordination to the will of Big Capital in the name of economic revival. This alliance came about after the Chilean coup and the oil crisis of 1973. The following years witnessed the rise, both financially and institutionally, of the chemical and energy sectors in world capitalism. After his release from prison, Massimo is seen walking on the beach; in the distance are the factories and oil refineries, belching smoke into the air. On the soundtrack we hear Massimo's voice: "Comrade Simonetti always said that things would change. But too much time has passed and we're doing worse than ever. I feel so lonely. I used to have my sister, but she's gone too...I feel like drowning myself, plunging my head into this ocean of oil." The rise of the chemical and energy sectors in world capitalism significantly impacted the worker's struggle toward socialization and resulted in layoffs, inflation, and chronic unemployment. Massimo would eventually end up doing the very work that, in his words "robs you of all joy," becoming simply a cog in the great machine of capitalism.

Moving slightly beyond the time period in the film which ends in 1972, I'll mention that as a result of the 1976 elections, the PCI had increased its voting strength but was not strong enough to substantiate a Leftist government. It needed the help of the Christian Democrats. Thus, the "Historical Compromise"[1] ended up bolstering the weakening Christian Democratic party. For the Italian workers, this meant paying for the economic downturn that grew worse in the years between 1973-1976 due to the oil crisis. There were consumer restrictions and reduced spending. Living conditions worsened and there was growing distrust of unions. Unemployment reached staggering proportions in 1977, with close to two million people out of work. Conditions did not improve in Italy despite the initial promises of the Communist Party in the post-war years. The emerging capitalist domination of Italy and Germany, for that matter, was just beginning. Vittoria intuits the possibilities in embracing American Capital. Massimo remains a Communist, despite his sense that their original impulse was barely felt anymore. During this time of increasing inflation, we notice that even the French prostitute's prices have gone up from 500 lire to 2000 lire.

Continuing with some of the historical details and concluding with Schroeter's comments on the period: On March 7, 1977 the student movement took over Bologna (a stronghold of the PCI) and Rome. There was violent conflict in Rome. Five days later, Rome became the stage of a six-hour battle including thousands of youths. During the following days, the movement invaded the city of Bologna. The PCI's ability to maintain public order was undermined and the state resorted to brutal repression throughout Italy. Hundreds were arrested in Bologna and elsewhere, radio stations were closed, journals and magazines

---

1   The "Historical Compromise" referred to an alliance between the Christian Democrats and the Italian Communist Party. This alliance came about after the Chilean coup and the oil crisis of 1973. The following years witnessed the rise, both financially and institutionally, of the chemical and energy sectors in world capitalism. This significantly impacted the workers' struggle toward socialization and resulted in layoffs, inflation, and chronic unemployment. At the same time the Chilean experience exposed the deficiency of old models of socialist government.

confiscated, bookstores shut down. Franco Berardi writes about this period:

> Now one began to discover that social democracy, even though introducing new elements into the communist worker movement tradition of the Third International, was not necessarily in contradiction with totalitarian, violent and Stalinist trends. In fact, the two aspects were mixed in the PCI, which had become a component of bourgeoisie democracy by abandoning every type of violence against the existing order [while] at the same time [maintaining the] violent force of totalitarianism against the revolutionary movement.

It was clear that the movement was in crisis. As a collective, it could not reconcile its member's ideals with the growing violence and state repression. Armed warfare had begun to take center stage, eventually engulfing the entire movement.

The Red Brigade had grown from the workers' struggle in the early years of the '70s. This militant faction came from factories in Milan, Turin, and Genoa. At first, kidnapping of factory managers and acts of sabotage were linked with the workers' struggle. But soon, they would break with the movement and develop into an aggressive militant organization against the state. Their clandestine operations culminated with the kidnapping and murder of Aldo Moro, President of the Christian Democrats. Schroeter had the following to say about this time in Italy:

> I saw the political events of the year 1977, during what is known as the German Autumn [referring to the arrest and death of members of the RAF in jail which resulted to widespread repression in Germany], from the Italian point of view. The Red Brigades who were operating in that country might call themselves anarchists, but we had every reason to regard them as modern fascists. The former prime minister of Italy, Aldo Moro, was abducted and murdered in the

spring of 1978, when *The Kingdom of Naples* came out. Moro was a right-wing politician of the Democrazi Christiana party, in favor of a "historic compromise" with the Italian Communists, and had wanted to involve them in government in order to surmount the economic crisis. Today we can be fairly sure of what was rumored then, that the secret services, with the help of the CIA, had taken part in his murder in order to discredit the Communists and destabilize the country. We were all discussing it openly at the premiere of *The Kingdom of Naples* in Cannes.

In this political climate, Massimo is looking not only for direction in life but love. As a young man, he procured business for the French prostitute and in return received a portion of the profit. When he is in the town square attempting to sell the Communist newspaper, *l'Unità,* he sees her in the distance, running but not running away from two sailors who accost her. It is a kind of elaborate flirtation not without a sense of danger. Massimo is fascinated by her and wants the approval and love he was never able to receive from his mother, who died young. There is a scene where we see the French prostitute is standing and warming herself next to a fire, outside in the rain. Time has passed, she seems older, less well kept, and her beauty has faded. For the first time we see behind the scarlet curtain and it is no longer mysterious. Behind it, there is simply a grimy wall. Massimo is there and annoyed; we realize that this is after they had sex for the first time; he claims, "you treated me like a john…no kisses, no embraces." What he doesn't realize, of course, is that she is not capable of giving him the love that he desires. He is also annoyed because she took his money after sex, so she gives it back to him. He throws it onto the ground in anger. His sister also threw away the money that Mrs. Ferrante gave her, while visiting her mother's grave; for brother and sister it is "dirty" money. Massio is seen walking away from the prostitute; but suddenly, he turns around and embraces her and cries out, "I love you, I love you." He is in tears. She tells him: "Don't cry. You're young. You have the light. I'm hidden in the darkness…

darker and darker…older and older." We sense that Massimo's father loved his mother, but she died young. Caviola remarries Simonetti, a man younger than herself and eventually murders him, because she holds him responsible for her daughter's death. In the end, she is committed to an insane asylum. Vittoria does not suffer for love but pursues her studies instead and lands a job working in a hotel.

In *The Kingdom of Naples,* music plays an important role just as in all of Schroeter's films. Here he uses popular tunes, Neapolitan folk songs, and revolutionary songs as well as opera. There is one scene in the film where he uses music ironically to comment on the images. Early in the film, Caviola prostitutes her daughter, Rosa, to a Black American GI for a bag of wheat from America. As we see him enter the apartment and approach Rosa, we hear the song (whose lyrics are racist) "Tammurriata Nera," a Neapolitan song written in 1944 by E.A. Mario (music) and Edoardo Nicolardi (text). Here it is sung by Roberto Murolo, who helped make it famous throughout the world. The song tells of a young woman who had given birth to a child of color and how the people are shocked and begin to gossip about the possible father. The frequent Fassbinder actor, Günther Kaufmann, was the child of just such an arrangement in the post-war years. Nicolardi was inspired to write the song based on an episode that happened to him: he witnessed a certain uproar in the maternity ward at the Naples Loreto Mare hospital, of which he was the administrative manager. We hear the lyrics tell of "wheat that will grow where it is sown" during a close-up of Caviola's hand grasping a bag of wheat on which is written in bold letters, U.S.A. Opera also contributes, along with gesture and bodily movement, to heighten the drama of Rosa's death scene. Vittoria starts singing in order to make the day pass quicker as she scrubs the floor; music emerges from suffering. Caviola breaks out into song at the after-party for her marriage; her performance is raw, off-key, and filled with histrionic gestures. Music is often used in this film to add another layer to the drama; it is never merely background music for Schroeter but as essential to the film as its images.

Massimo and Vittoria have a conversation after visiting Mrs. Cavioli in the insane asylum that reflects their individual states of mind. They are both grown up and Vittoria has become a realist. After witnessing Mrs. Cavioli, she tells Massimo that: "now you can understand the sadness of our community." She goes on to speak of their mother and Comrade Simonetti who are now dead, of how the attorney Palumbo betrayed them and joined the Christian Democrats, and finally how Rosa died due to complications from pneumonia. Prompted by thoughts of her brother's future, she asks him: "What happens when the few cents you get from the party are no longer enough?" She implores him: "Massimo, open your eyes! Don't be a dreamer all your life." He responds: "Vittoria, you're right, but I still believe in the party. Comrade Simonetti's death must not be in vain." They are not heartfelt words, but platitudes he learned from a Party that he does not see has betrayed him. Vittoria then displays sisterly affection in order to change the subject and teases him about "Rosaria," the French prostitute. She is naïve about sex. He tells her she is older now and can barely stand up. He is being truthful, but she says that she doesn't believe him laughing and teasing him further. It is a poignant moment in the film where we see the bond of sibling affection struggling to find common ground in a changing world.

Massimo is stuck in the past and uses words that no longer have meaning. Vittoria looks to the future and to the emerging capitalist economy that would eventually come to dominate all facets of life in Italy. She is like the young girl who desires to escape her small-town life by attending a University in a big city. Massimo is like the young man whose attachment to people and events from the past keep him from seeing the possibilities for a better life beyond it. This is why he is so devastated at the end of the film when he sees "Frenchie" during the carnival season; she is no longer what she once was; she is older now and no longer as beautiful and lovely. She doesn't seem to even recognize him. Blood is dripping from her mouth and collapses onto the floor. She is one person he felt a kind of love for and represents and connection to the past. He screams "Help, Help" and these are the final words of the film. Schroeter wanted to show how with "the American occupation, and subsequent string-pulling" and the "establishment of the Christian Democrats and the Communist Party...the poor were the losers all along the line."

As suggested above, *The Kingdom of Naples* is a stylist departure from Schroeter's earlier films wrote. He writes:

> The idea for *The Kingdom of Naples* came to me in 1975/76, after I had exhausted all my stylistic mannerisms and fought all my battles with myself and my personal genius in *Flocons D'or*. That period was over, and I was in search of a new departure. When I felt that I could go no farther in the underground cinema, I thought of Naples. I wanted a period that I could confidently survey and the elements of a family saga reaching from 1945 to 1972. I wrote the scenario and created an extended version with the beautiful photographs I had taken in Naples and its surroundings.

Of course, he didn't completely abandon his mannerist style. *The Kingdom of Naples* is staged like a drama in sixteen acts rather than a linear film; for example, there are great leaps in time that occur throughout the film. Its structure is not epic like Visconti's in *The Leopard* but condensed like a history play by Shakespeare made for the screen. It contains instances of "bad" but intensely emotional singing, dramatic death scenes underscored by opera, histrionic gestures, and stylized movements; all the qualities that make a Schroeter film unique.

In the following quote, Gerd Gemünden, talks about Schroeter's relation to politics and the form of his film. Alluding to Rosa von Pranheim's criticism of the *The Kingdom of Naples,* he writes, "what Praunheim is really furious about is Schroeter's unwillingness to support the kind of gay activism that he himself embodies. The deeper nature of this rift clearly indicates that the two filmmakers define the political in very different ways. In contrast to von Praunheim's activism, Schroeter favors an approach in which the form itself is political — these are not films about politics, but political filmmaking."

Schroeter visited Naples when he was sixteen years old and stayed for a year. He fell in love with the surroundings and with the many Southern dialects that we hear in his films. In Naples, Schroeter experienced a way of life very different from the one in Germany. Karsten Witte speaks of this relationship between Italy and Germany in Schroeter's films: "in almost all of his films, Schroeter almost obsessively depicts the contradiction between the empire of freedom (Italy) and the empire of necessity (Germany), under which he suffers." His film, *Palermo or Wolfsburg,* examines this relation in greater detail. The title "Kingdom of Naples" refers to the time prior to Garibaldi's conquest of Italy and Naples in 1860 and yet Schroeter's film is about the port city from 1945 to 1972. But for Schroeter it doesn't matter whether we are speaking of a monarchy, a dictatorship, or a republic: time is cyclical. There is no progress, no movement towards a better future, only the endless repetition of poverty, misery, and death; even though fascism has been replaced by communism and capitalism, there is never any benefit for the poor. Only the Church seems to remain in a fixed relation to the world. I have said that Vittoria is one who seems to emerge from the wreckage of the post war years with hope for the future. But she, as all the others in the film, does not see yet the full impact of global capitalism. Perhaps Massimo is right when he says that he feels she is sad and lonely in her new position. There is that scene on the beach, near the end of the film, where Massimo gives a salute and then there is a cut to the scene of his sister giving a salute as a stewardess, then a cut back to Massimo still giving a salute. It is one of those wonderful touches by Schroeter. Do they somehow communicate over vast distances as a result of the cutting of the film? Are they more like each other than they are aware, despite their different positions in life? Years later, when Schroeter was taking stock of his films, he reflected and wrote about *The Kingdom of Naples*:

After my mother's death, I looked back on my films, taking stock. I couldn't stop at that, fond as I was of them all. *The Kingdom of Naples* was more accessible, less subversive, but

I felt good about it because the people in Naples had confirmed my own feelings. Previously, I had been more absorbed in myself, but I couldn't go on identifying with youth forever [as Massimo does in the film]. Ten years after 1968, I was looking for a new way to ask the basic questions by which I stand to this day: How can the power of death be broken? How can we love human beings with all their contradictions? Many who were close to me could not accept the way I linked these questions with criticisms of political circumstances. The team working on *The Kingdom of Naples* confirmed my belief that I had understood the situation and mentality of the Neapolitans surprisingly well, and that approval seemed to me more valuable than all the outspoken criticisms of my style.

The Kingdom of Naples would go on to win a major prize at the Taormina Film Festival.

Works Cited

Berardi, Franco. "Anatomy of Autonomy." In *Autonomia: Post-Political Politics,* edited by Sylvère Lotringer and Christian Marazzi, 148–70. Los Angeles: Semiotext(e), 2007.

Gemünden, Gerd. "Werner Schroeter's Italian Journeys." In *Werner Schroeter,* edited by Roy Grudmann, 126–39. Vienna: Österreichisches Filmmuseum; Synema-Gesellschaft für Film und Medien, 2018.

Schroeter, Werner, and Claudia Lenssen. *Days of Twilight, Nights of Frenzy.* Translated by Anthea Bell. Chicago: University of Chicago Press, 2017.

9

A Sicilian in Germany:
On Werner Schroeter's *Palermo*
or Wolfsburg (1980)

Giovanna to Nicola: "You must ask Lady Volkswagen: 'Where shall I work'"

In Werner Schroeter's *Palermo or Wolfsburg,* the scene shifts from Naples (*The Kingdom of Naples*) to Sicily as it follows the fates of the members of the Zarbo family: Nicola and his younger brother, Caruso, his father Liddru[1], and his uncle. They confront the fact that Nicola is leaving for Germany to make money so his father could buy land in Southern Italy. Many people from Italy left for Germany during the 1970s to pursue work in a country that was rebuilt with American money and adopted its brand of corporate capitalism. Sicily, as it's portrayed in the first part of the film, which is in the style of Italian neo-realism, is a region of poetry, music, joy, humor as well as the despair caused by the poverty, and housing problems.[2] A builder tells

---

1 Nicola's mother died from childbed fever.
2 Liddru, Nicola and Caruso's father, wants to buy land from a rich land-owner who charges a large price for it. Caruso's father can't afford it. This is one of the reasons why Nicola goes to Germany; he wants to make money so his father can afford the land. Caruso asks his father, "Tell me the story

Nicola early in the film that the houses are not finished because the money ran out. But there is a kind of acceptance of life. The difference between a Southern and Northern sensibility is reflected early in the film in the scene between two young Sicilian men over a game of pool. For one, Germany exploits its workers, makes them slaves of Capitalism; he says that Sicilians need to take risks and make their own work instead of being slaves of a master. The other contends that in Germany there is greater freedom and the ability to find work and have fun on the weekends. It's a sentiment that will be echoed by the young gay man on the train to Germany, who tells Nicola that he has to go to Germany because he feels that there is more freedom to do what one wants there. What he means, but refrains from telling Nicola, but not Giovanni, is that he believes in Germany he is more free as a gay man. The difference between the South and North will be developed throughout the film and lead to tragic results.

Before he leaves, Nicola consults a priest and an older eccentric baron.[3] They both emphasize that he must think of his family and do the right thing. In their own way they also underline that Germany is a foreign country, and that the people there are not like him. Their subtle message is that, as an immigrant in a foreign country, he must find a way to integrate himself. The priest also tells him that the moral standards of the Germans are not up to the standards of Italians, with their center in the Roman Catholic Church and the family. As the

---

about the Master [the rich landowner] and his beautiful house." Liddru responds: "The Master's grandfather worked there [on the land] as a simple peasant. His great-grandfather, too. His ancestors were all peasants. They went into the fields with weapons and guarded everything. The almond trees, the beans, everything." The Mafia was also a problem in the South. In another scene, Liddru and Caruso are seen walking toward the church. Caruso asks him if all men are equal; his father responds yes; Caruso then asks his father if he is equal to the Master; Liddru is silent.

3   Schroeter said of this character: "The strange baron in the film was a genuine aristocrat from an old Palma di Montechiaro family. We changed nothing about his curious way of life; he really did live, surrounded by china figurines, in the crazy mountain village shown in the film, thought himself widely travelled and gave Nicola advice."

priest speaks the words, "avoid harmful company and by that, I mean especially the women who have already caused so much sorrow," we see on the screen men carrying a statue of the Virgin Mary with many bills stuffed in her hands. It is a complex montage; on the one hand there is the Virgin, on the other there is the German woman Nicola falls in love with whose name is Brigette. But there is the added complication of money, the suggestion of a whore; during the trial, Schroeter inserts a scene of Brigette nude as a stripper in one of those peepshows that were popular in the '70s; Nicola watches her from behind the glass. The combination of Virgin Mary, the Roman Catholic Church, money, prostitution, capitalism create a provocative series of associations.

The other person who once was a part-time prostitute is Giovanna, the present owner of a bar, who helped Nicola when he first arrived in Germany. In an attempt to embarrass Giovanna, and invalidate her testimony, the prosecutor brings up the time in her life when she was a prostitute. She counters by saying she was a prostitute in big German cities, suggesting that she had many important and wealthy clients just like the prosecutor. And she sarcastically tells him that she made more money than he did. In the film, she is the example of a strong, confident woman who will not be swayed by German law, unlike Brigitte, who is a young woman unsure of what she wants. When Hans and his buddy Gustav get rowdy in her bar, she breaks a bottle and uses it to slash Gustav's lip. Once again, Schroeter used the great diva, Ida Di Benedetto — who played Mrs. Ferrante in *The Kingdom of Naples* — to play the part of Giovanna.

One night, before he left for Germany, Nicola rises from his bed, exits from the glass door in his bedroom and goes out onto the balcony, disappearing into the darkness. He is holding a postcard with an image of a church; he lights a match so he can see it clearly in the dark. Then there is a cut to a dream sequence, where Nicola is seen emerging from the Church; the Church as well as Nicola are bathed in a lurid red glow. There is a subsequent cut to Nicola blowing out the light and the screen grows dark. This image of the church will reappear during the trial. During the Passion Play, scenes of which appear during the film, there is a scene of the Last Supper; Thomas is given the wine to drink from but after taking a sip he spits it out and pours the wine on the ground, saying "to me it is full of bitterness." Thomas is also bathed in that lurid red light, distinct from the rest of the Apostles who are under a bright light and clearly visible. Is Nicola a Christ figure or a figure of Lucifer, i.e., with darker drives? Perhaps, it is better to say that he embodies both aspects. Near the end of the film, Christ is crucified on the cross and Thomas hangs himself. In the spiritual sense, Nicola becomes a Christ figure when he first arrives in Germany. Hans and Gustav persecute him by calling him racist names like "Dago" and making other offensive comments based on his immigrant status. As an immigrant Nicola is immediately demonized; but if he's called a dog, he'll bite. His immigrant status is brought up by Brigette's mother at the trial, where she constantly repeats, during her testimony, the words, "But he doesn't even speak German. You know what I mean?" And in a sense, Nicola does "hang" himself when he says, even though he was found innocent, about the murder, "I killed them, and I wanted to kill them." What is clear is that rather than playing the victim, he admits the truth and accepts the consequences brought about by his true nature, complex and demonic.

There is also the scene with Franco Bellia, a friend of Nicola's father, who was his contact in Germany when he arrived: when Franco's German wife appears and questions the presence of Nicola at the door, who had even told Franco that he would be willing to sleep in a garage, Franco goes back on his promise to help; his final gesture before asking Nicola to leave is to give him some money despite his wife's protests. As Franco speaks imperfect German at the trial, we hear the people snickering in the background; we are reminded that he was also an immigrant and he himself was unable to assimilate and instead became submissive to the will of his German wife. The poor are defeated by Capitol. He will try to divert the attention from himself since he does not want to be known as someone who was willing to help Nicola. The moral: an Italian in a foreign country will lose his sense of brotherhood with fellow Italians and will betray another Italian. Germany's relation to Italy was complex at this time. We hear on the television in Brigette's home that Germany is threatening to stop their aid to Italy if there are still Communists in the country. Brigette's mother, hearing this, exclaims: "Italian Communists. That's the absolute limit! Now Germany has to finance Italian Communists. I'm not working to pay for that." During the '70s, Italian and German politics were in turmoil.

In the early 1970s the worker's movement in Italy gained a base on the national level, participating in elections and distancing itself from the old forms of policy making. The discussion in Italy was now directly engaged with political issues, the central one being the "problem of power." In May 1973, "Worker's Power" dissolved and split into two groups. One went underground and grew increasingly militant eventually becoming the Red Brigade. The other group with Antonio Negri,[4] Franco Piperno,[5] and Oreste Scalzone,[6] went on to create the extra-parliamentary Autonomist movement. The refusal of the PCI (the Italian

4   The Marxist sociologist and political philosopher Antonio Negri wrote many influential books urging "revolutionary consciousness." He was arrested with many others in 1979 and accused of being the leader of the Red Brigade and actively participating in the murder of Aldo Moro, president of the Christian Democrats. Voice evidence suggested Negri made a threatening phone call on behalf of the Red Brigade. But this, along with many other accusations, was later dropped. He fled to France where for many years he taught alongside Jacques Derrida, Michel Foucault, and Gilles Deleuze.

5   Italian Communist. He was active in the 1968 movement and in 1969 took part in the demonstrations against Fiat in Turin. With Negri and Oreste Scalzone he was charged in 1979 for the publication of subversive magazines but escaped arrest. In 1981 he was convicted to 10 years imprisonment for participation in the kidnapping of Aldo Moro. Most of the charges were later dropped and the sentence reduced.

6   A Marxist intellectual and co-founder with Negri and Piperno of the Autonomy movement. In March 1968, his vertebral column was seriously injured by a desk thrown from a window by neo-fascists at a University in Rome. In 1979 he was arrested with Negri and Piperno and accused of plotting attacks to overthrow the government.

Communist party) and the Christian Democrats to recognize this split, caused members of Autonomy to be accused of acts of terror that they in fact condemned. They were a true mass movement comprised of students, the unemployed, and those living on the margins of society. They came into increasing conflict with the PCI as a result of the Historical Compromise that dictated that Italy must be governed by an institutionalized political agreement with the Christian Democrats. The test came in the spring of 1975 when members fought with fascists and police in Rome. The wave of violence spread to Milan where a young fascist was killed as well as members of the police force. Thousands of factory workers joined the students and the unemployed. The inner city was under siege. There were riots and demonstrations. In Turin, a young Fiat worker was killed by an armed guard.

During this same time in Germany, the RAF, also known as the Baader-Meinhof gang, had kidnapped and assassinated prominent political and business figures in an attempt to incite an aggressive response from the government, an action that members believed would ignite a broader revolutionary movement. The RAF characterized the West German government as a fascist holdover from the Nazi era. As RAF's strategies became more violent it lost much of the support it had enjoyed among the West German political Left. By the mid-1970s the group had expanded its scope outside West Germany and occasionally allied itself with militant Palestinian groups. For example, in 1976 two Baader-Meinhof guerrillas took part in a Palestinian hijacking of an Air France jetliner, which eventually ended after the successful Entebbe raid in Uganda by Israeli commandos. Both Italy and Germany were facing problems brought on by radical terrorist organizations. In the film, Antonio's ideas are a result of the political tensions in Italy and Germany in the 70s.

Of Nicola's Italian friends in Germany, Antonio is the most vocal in terms of what he thinks is the solution to the capitalist problem (the problem of power) and his ideas are the most radical; his words could have been said by a member of the Red Brigade or the RAF: "You can't change this society, this infallible society. All you can do is destroy it. That man is a boss. The factory belongs to him. Take a gun and shoot him." Finally, he says the Volkswagen building, where both he and Nicola work, should be blown up. Nicola responds: "Can you really do that?" Antonio says: "I'm obsessed with the idea." After both Nicola and Antonio witness two men carrying a hearse with a veiled woman walking in front of them, Nicola asks her who has died. The woman tells him and Antonio that her husband died in an accident, presumably in a factory. They learn she wants to bury him in Italy. Antonio tells Nicola: "Now you see how healthy life is here." Antonio's comments are the result of seeing the life workers from Italy had to face in Germany, both at the Volkswagen factory and in their living arrangements. Werner Schroeter writes:

> …the conditions to which living in the workers' hostels in Germany had to adjust were terrible. They tried to keep some of the culture of their homeland going by gambling and throwing parties — fueled by plenty of alcohol, of course. What else were they to do? Although they wore ear protectors, their hearing was damaged by the noise of the conveyor belts and the incredibly loud machinery. Their jobs sometimes took them from the cradle to the grave — a wretched life.

And in such an environment love cannot blossom.

Nicola first meets Brigette on his second day in Germany; he had spent the night in the bushes next to the mechanics shop where she works. Noticing him, she immediately teases him and then throughout the course of trying to understand each other's different language, she comes to realize he is Sicilian. The cultural and linguistic differences cause Nicola to misread Brigette's gestures and motivations. In his room, he writes letters home in which he tells his father that he is in engaged. We find out that Brigette, who is barely sixteen years old, is manipulating Nicola to play Gustav against Hans. At the country fair she reads his enthusiastic displays of love as the gestures of a kind of madman, because of their cultural differences, and runs away from him into the arms of Gustav. He has been betrayed and is confused. We soon discover that Brigitte has also abandoned Hans and Gustav and it is precisely at the moment when they want to be his friends and offer to buy him a drink, that Nicola, unable to understand them, misreads their gestures as aggressive, and, in anger, stabs and kills both of them. Antonio arrives and sees what his friend had done and tells Nicola to leave the scene, but he doesn't and prefers to kneel, his hands folded in prayer, in front of the dead bodies. Before he leaves, Antonio tears two wooden stakes from the fence near the bodies and throws them on the ground; he will later testify that he witnessed Hans and Gustav attack Antonio with the stakes thus provoking his self-defense. It is a lie that Antonio will maintain even when questioned in court. Nicola, facing the dead bodies, looks up at the night sky. At moments during the trial, he will also fold his hands, extending his arms outward, in prayer, while gazing upward. The idea of a Catholic God is so branded on the consciousness of a young Italian and penetrates all the aspects of his life. With tears in his eyes, he will eventually accept his punishment before God, but also in a sense, in defiance of God; he is tense when he prays, not at peace. Carly Flinn writes, "If it seems odd for Schroeter to create an angel in standard Christian, religious, and (German) legal terms, it must be noted that he bypasses both religion and nationalism in making a murderer that 'angel,' extending a beatification of Nicola's integrity rather than an act of Christian and legal forgiveness." I would further contend that such integrity is also mixed with pride, a Luciferian pride.

In her testimony, Giovanna emphasizes the difference between a Southern Italian sensibility and a Northern German one. She tells the court, speaking of an immigrant's life in Germany: "In this land without light, without sun, without songs, without chatter...there is nothing for us here but work...we are two different worlds." She speaks the following lines while facing directly at the camera (i.e., addressing Nicola): "You understand as little about us as we do about you. Only we don't need to understand you. As we don't want anything from you. We live in different worlds." But she might as well be directing the words to the audience viewing the film who would have initially been Germans. It is a provocative rejection of life in German and an assertion of the essential *differences* between the Southern and Northern sensibilities. The Lay Assessor attempts to divert attention from Giovanna's testimony and cautions everyone that we must "find the truth." He makes a connection between poverty and crime, saying that aggression arises from the differences between desire and benefit, and that Nicola is a product of these "not so idyllic" surroundings of poverty. The Lay Assessor tries to deflate Giovanna's argument by referring to her comments about the beauty of sun and sea as commonplace statements, clichés. Giovanna responds: "Sun and sea are facts, aren't they?...And if you want to mention culture and aggression we have never started a war...we were often attacked but we have remained the same: human beings. Sadness is not a crime. He [Nicola] is no murderer, he is sad." Schroeter is militant in refusing to accept German law and justice, a holdover from the Nazi era, and is clearly on the side of the immigrant. Gerd writes (p. 139): "Nicola's admission of guilt is a refusal of the victim role, a refusal of letting others determine what one is or is not — a rare position in German films from this period." At one point, the judge tries to put a stop to what he calls the displays of Italian emotion. Ironically, and rather humorously, the slain boys' mothers protest that they should also be allowed to express their emotions as Germans. In an excessive manner, typical of Schroeter, the one mother, aroused by the sight of Brigette's naked breasts, turns to kiss the other; the other runs out of the courtroom, horrified. Of course, Schroeter has always valued the intensity of passion in a performance rather than perfection.

Critics have spoken of *Palermo or Wolfsburg* as being in three parts: the neorealist first part, the scenes in Germany as the second part; and the courtroom sequence as the third part. The music varies in the film whether we are in Sicily or in Germany. In the south, Schroeter uses regional songs and opera. There are also those wonderfully humorous scenes with the frustrated opera teacher, who alternately tries to teach a young man to sing in high C, defends the works of Bellini while lamenting what he sees as the narrowness of the Italian musical scene, and with his friend concocts a plan to create an airport in Sicily to increase tourism. It is a delightfully mad idea! He is a wild dreamer, obsessed with opera, and with an impossible vision. He sings a song early in the film while tapping on his guitar whose lines, "I call life, and death answers me" foreshadow the tragic event in the film. I imagine him as a kind of reflection of Schroeter himself. Nicola's uncle in the film is just as important a minor character, who is seen at the beginning of the film writing poetry. He responds to Liddru that he likes "to write love poetry" to pass the time and so as to "think no evil." The older friend of Liddru, who talks with him at the bar, recites to him a poem about hope that he wrote while in prison. The South is rich with song and poetry.

In Germany, the soundtrack changes: there is no melody, no passion, the mechanical and repetitive sounds of the factory dominate the soundtrack. These are the sounds of the large factories and oil refineries whose only function was to exploit the workers from 9 to 5. Schroeter has said that the structure of the Volkswagen building resembles a concentration camp. At the music fair, the contestant from Braunshweig chooses to sing, "Zwei kleine Italiener" (Two Little Italians), a song by Connie Froebess, "who sang this song as the 1962 Germany entry to the Eurovision Song Contest." As she sings off key, her voice cracking on the higher notes, and wearing a colorful, almost psychedelic dress, Schroeter cuts to Nicola, after Brigette has left him, walking toward the exit where the symbol of Volkswagen is reflected onto his face. The song is, of course, not exactly about being welcome. The refection of the symbol on Nicola's face suggests that he is under the spell of certain economic and cultural forces that he has no control over and that destroy his chances for love in Germany. Schroeter is unambiguous here: backbreaking and repetitive work in a factory kills the soul.

During the courtroom scenes, we hear Alban Berg's Violin Concerto, but there are also interesting sound effects that Schroeter uses. In particular, when Brigitte's mother is giving her testimony, her gestures are excessive and her delivery histrionic. She is clearly an absurd character who at points in her testimony suggests that Nicola's inability to speak German marks him as an inferior immigrant. At one point her voice is sped up on the soundtrack and sounds more like a deranged bird call than a human voice. But there is also the scene where Nicola, after leaving the music fair, is walking at night and playing the harmonica. Of course, the harmonica is often associated with folk or blues music. In general, we see characters in Schroeter's films resorting to listening or playing music or singing (as well as writing poetry) as a way to cope with their suffering.

Like the music, the general color tone of each section of the film also varies. In Sicily, colors are vibrant in the landscape and in the young men's dress; Schroeter's camera lingers on the great expanse of the green countryside; the opera teacher's elegant clothes, the oranges and reds of the young men's jeans, instead of the American blue jeans, everything is highlighted under a bright sun. It is a land rich in tradition, both Catholic and Pagan. Also, in the opening of the film, we see a group of excited boys running out of a building into the sun-drenched countryside. That excitement and enthusiasm, that passion, is essential to the Southern sensibility. In Germany, the dominant color is the gray of the Volkswagen building, which sets the emotional tone of the film. Gone is the vast countryside, the bright sun; here there is the smoke from the factories, the dull-colored and empty rooms of the workers, the overall dim lighting as though it is always approaching night; the sky is ominous over the factory. In the courtroom sequence night has arrived. The light is sinister and dark; there is the dominant black of the robes of the lawyers and judges; the overwhelming sense is of controlled gestures instead of passionate emotion.[7] That is, before the formal

---

7   Schroeter writes about the courtroom: "We shot the closing sequence of
      the film, the courtroom scene, in Berlin. Our location, the building on the

proceedings descend into chaos, where repressed desires are given free reign against the dominance of the Law.

There is one exception to this sinister light and that is the open window in the courtroom which opens out on the bright sun reflecting on a building; it is the one link to the outside world. In the scenes that conclude the film, we see a close-up of Nicola's face, framed by darkness; only the right side of his face is illuminated. He hears a disembodied voice from the open window that repeats "touch me, touch me," and the film ends on this note; it is as if the bright light is eroticized, yielding a voice that calls for permission to touch a body. Schroeter writes: "At the end of the film I speak to the viewers, off camera, appealing to them: 'Touch one another, touch one another.'" He continues:

> I had the feeling that, in Germany, personal contact was un-
> thinkable. Today, when everyone moves around in virtual
> space, the sheer oddity of it, our inability to make physical
> contact with other people, seems even greater.

Giovanna tells the jury that Nicola is sad, and in one sense, she means: desire thwarted and repressed leads to sadness. Passion can also be aggressive and voyeuristic. The scene in the court-room where Nicola tears Brigette's blouse, exposing her naked breasts, verges on surreal because prior to this event Nicola sees Brigette dancing naked in a Wolfsburg peepshow. These are the only sexually explicit moments in the film; but here permission is thwarted by emotional misreadings, the result of a difference in language and culture. In Antonio's testimony we hear him espouse a way of life more in line with radical desire than global capitalism.

When Antonio first enters the courtroom, he runs to Nicola and passionately embraces and kisses him until he's pulled off

---

Reichpietschufer, had been the Nazi People's Court. The scene we were shooting took place on the very spot where the fanatical Nazi judge Ro-land Freisler passed death sentences. At the time, the building still radiated that atmosphere; today the historical effect seems to have been blotted out by modern renovation."

him. He immediately refuses to answer a question from the prosecutor. As a result, we hear someone among those common people who attended the trial yell, "fascist." It is an ironic and absurd statement. Then Antonio is asked, "Tell me your opinion of private property, of justice, of human life, of values?" He responds: "I am a human being, a man, a son, a friend, a brother. But perhaps I'm an anarchist, too." He is asked: "and private property?" Antonio responds: "I have none. Why should I?" Then the jurors agree he should be sworn in. So he is asked: "Do you want to swear by God or not." Antonio asks: "Can I swear by the bones of my mother." The sarcastic reply: "We don't have them here." He makes the gesture with his index and middle fingers called "flicking the V's" which means "piss off," as he responds: "I won't swear by God." His delivery is confident, even when he lies about what he saw the night of the murders, in order to protect Nicola whom he loves. His facial expressions are simultaneously filled with anger and sadness. It is the sadness and anger of a man, like Nicola, who is drawn into a foreign culture, by economic necessity, a country that represses radical desire, and makes one into a robot working the machine of capitalism, all the while experiencing increased anxiety and worry to the extent that one loses one's mind[8], as did the older man, Giovanni, who worked in the Volkswagen factory for many years.

There was to be a third firm in the trilogy, after *The Kingdom of Naples* and *Palermo or Wolfsburg*, dealing the situation in Italy, and it was to be titled *Italia — Speranza de futuro?* (Italy — Hope for the future?). About this project, Schroeter wrote: "At the time I believed in the utopian idea that, because of its people, its quality of life, and its sense of liberty, Italy could still be a model for Europe as a whole. I gave that hope up long ago, and as a result the third film in what would have been a trilogy, a journey through Italy in the style of the commedia dell'arte, was never made. I cleaned the makeup off the subject's face, so to speak, and forgot Italy."

---

8   About Giovanni, Antonio tells Nicola, pointing to him: "You see that man. Is he still a person? They have driven him insane."

Nevertheless, as the record of a time and place, *The King-dom of Naples* and *Palermo or Wolfsburg*, remain evocative and powerful testaments of the beauty and culture of Italy, as well as its Southern people. The films transcend their subject matter, as high art, and rival even the best of those films that emerged from that movement called Italian Neo-Realism. Schroeter fell in love with the South of Italy when he visited it for the first time when he was six years old; he fell in love with the language and especially the various Southern dialects. He was fluent in Italian and served as interpreter for Pasolini, a director he admired, when he showed *Accatone* in Heidelberg in 1961. *Palermo or Wolfsburg* was the first ever German film to win the Golden Bear at the Berlin Film Festival. The film was Schroeter's greatest success, added to which was the fact that he was responsible for the script, dialogue, make-up, and editing, and the film received enthusiastic reviews upon its release.

Works Cited

Gemünden, Gerd. "Werner Schroeter's Italian Journeys." In *Werner Schroeter,* edited by Roy Grudmann, 126–39. Vienna: Österreichisches Filmmuseum; Synema-Gesellschaft für Film und Medien, 2018.

Flinn, Caryl. "Werner Schroeter's Exotic Music and Margins." In *Werner Schroeter,* edited by Roy Grudmann, 106–25. Vienna: Österreichisches Filmmuseum; Synema-Gesellschaft für Film und Medien, 2018.

Schroeter, Werner, and Claudia Lenssen. *Days of Twilight, Nights of Frenzy.* Translated by Anthea Bell. Chicago: University of Chicago Press, 2017.

10

"I Want My Future": On Werner Schroeter's *Day of the Idiots* (1981)

"I had long been interested in Michel Foucault's *Madness and Civilization,* the *Anti-Oedipus* of Deleuze and Guattari, as well as the antipsychiatry writing of R.D. Laing, David Cooper, and Franco Basaglia. In Italy, the last named had succeeded in his demand to have mental hospitals opened and schizophrenics let out into the world. The philosophy and politics of that policy of opening such institutions interested me greatly, since homosexuals had also been defined as sick, people to be shut away and treated therapeutically — that repression, sanctioned by authority, was one reason why I rejected psychology, psychoanalysis, and psychiatry.

— Werner Schroeter

Werner Schroeter's *Tag der Idioten* (Day of the Idiots) (1981) is his bleakest film, a film where desire is ultimately frustrated and finds no place to breathe, either in the outside world or in the confines an insane asylum, despite the latter serving as a space in the film for acts of transgressive freedom. In the opening scenes, we see that Carole Schneider's (Carole Bouquet) relationship with her boyfriend Alexander is fraught with difficulties, with misreadings of each other's emotions. In the first scene, Carole, presumably after their making love, since she is naked as is Alexander who is asleep on the bed, says that she would like to cut a rectangle out of the top of his head so that she could peer inside to see if he loves her. Do we ever know for sure if we are loved? How can we know? Can we actually know another person, or is it rather a matter of constantly interpreting them, and thus subject to errors? Carole is desperately in love with Alexander. She wants him to notice her; but not only to look at her but to really *see* her.

Her passion drives her to a kind of madness: she angrily clears the table in their room of all the papers, books, and other items; she throws his records, carefully arranged on the floor, against the wall; she tears his clothing; she sits on the floor next to him as he sleeps and reads a book out loud about angels; she asks him if he is hungry and then storms out of the apartment, slamming the door, and screaming the word, "food." In another scene, she tells Alexander that he can "take anything he wants from her," and that "he just needs to ask." She is offering herself to him. She says this leaning against a wall and while not looking at him. She removes all his clothes in a fit of erotic passion until he is naked before her, then quickly moves away from him, grazing his penis with her hand. Her desire is so overwhelming that she is unable to voice it; it is as if she has no control over her body; passion drives her mad. Alexander, throughout her displays of passion, sits on the bed, silently flipping through papers; this is the world of documents, language, transaction, profit; he is a conformist. Carole's world is one of intense feeling, a desire, as the song in the film says, "to drown in a sea of love."

After leaving the apartment, Carole goes to a restaurant and orders "three Viennese coffees." Alexander is there. She wants him to really *see* her. She burns her lips as she takes a long sip of her coffee; she pours one of the drinks onto the table; she rubs the frothy cream onto her face; smears her lipstick. These are almost childlike gestures in an attempt to draw someone's attention; but they are also private and creatively anarchic. They are a riddle that defies interpretation.

Throughout the film, there are these moments where the viewer witnesses the extremely private and internal displays of passion and perhaps even despair, or self-loathing, of the main character. As Wold Wondratschek says, speaking about what he calls Schroeter's "heraldry of gestures" which are as if "signs of powerlessness" as well as madness, "what remains is the shock of realization and the elemental power of the yearning for love, which is always, somehow, as far as I remember, in a nose dive of disintegration."

While still in the restaurant, she goes to the bathroom, tosses the entire contents of her handbag into the toilet, and puts on her red skirt and purple blouse; she is in drag now. A different self emerges which is more brazen, confident, and yet, despite this, in pain. The young Carole Bourgeut bears a resemblance to a young Werner Schroeter; I believe this is why he cast her. From the moment when she has changed her clothes, I believe a viewer is meant to see her as a beautiful boy. Schroeter obscures her breasts, for example, when she is in the bath as she first enters the asylum; her body is positioned in such a way in the tub that she could be mistaken for a young man. And throughout most of the film she is dressed in the prison attire in which she looks like a young beautiful boy. Of course, I am not saying that one couldn't read the film from the point of view of an oppressed woman, unable to find an outlet for her desires; what I am pointing out is a different space through which to read the film; rather than she or he a more fruitful reading would be to break down the duality of gender and think of him or her.

Through movements of her body, Carole expresses her frustration with the world of real objects and men.[1] There is a moment, as she emerges from the bathroom, where through physi-

---

1 Schroeter, in his memoir, writes the following about Carole Bouquet: "I thought Carole incredibly beautiful…with a gray, sharp, tremendous erotic charge. After her parents' divorce, she had grown up with her taciturn, strict father. Without a mother, she hadn't known for a long time what femininity is or how to live. She was extremely shy, very serious, could hardly make conversation or look in the mirror. She hated it when people stared at her."

cal movement, she conveys a certain tension between her and the objects of the outside world. She stands on the opposite side of swinging doors; she swings the door open and watches it close, without herself moving; she repeats the action, still without moving. When she swings the door. Open for a third time, rather than passing through, she lets it fall against her, and then pushes it open. As she exits, she witnesses presumably two men, moving about, mysteriously behind two screens. The scene evokes the adult video arcade booths or lounges that contained glory holes and were especially associated with gay male culture. The men's features are not visible because of the various scratches on the screen. In anger, Carole kicks each screen. We hear the sound of bells and noise. In frustration, she says, "Please kill me" and then there is the image of Alexander in close-up. The entire sequence suggests an aggressive relation to objects and men. She could have easily passed through the swinging doors but she doesn't; it is a way of challenging the ease with which people pass through spaces and life; she expresses the difficulty she has in navigating the space of familiar gesture and life in the outside world, i.e., as a gay man or woman and a transvestite; and who are these mysterious figures behind the screens; are they to her a reminder of Alexander's rejection of her passionate advances? Do they represent the patriarchy? Wolf Wondratschek: "Much in [Schroeter's] films remains invisible." *Day of the Idiots* resists interpretation and psychological explanation. We are not given enough information; man is a riddle without a solution. In the above examples, Schroeter is allowing us into Carole's private spaces, and we see her there committing acts of creative anarchy with relation to the real world.

After she has transformed herself, we see her in a large, lavishly decorated house. We are once again in a private space. Day of the Idiots contains some of the most exquisite displays of interior emotional spaces. For example, we see her blow the water out of the bowl that a small statue is holding; she enjoys the sudden spray of drops. She'll repeat the action later in the bathroom of the insane asylum; there, she will cup the water in her hand and blow into her palm, creating a spray of drops that she will then wipe from the mirror as she gazes at herself. She looks puzzled as if she is asking herself: who am I really? She moves up the stairs with her head leaning over, and a long ponytail swinging in front of her face. Then there is an exquisite closeup of her face and a single tear falling from her left eye. Prior to this, she lifted the needle of the record-player. Her fingers are oddly placed on the tone arm and her fingernails are painted scarlet; there is a close-up of her hand; she rubs her middle finger across the length of the tone arm, sexually suggestive, and then, instead of slowly and gently positioning the needle onto the record groove, she drops it. We hear a scratch and some static, before the music begins. It is a Dvořák trio which we will hear again in the psychiatrist, Dr. Bruno's office. It is an anarchic gesture against perfection; it is intentional but irrational, awkward, a "bad performance"; the scratch as noise is as important as the music; so too is passion more important than regulated desire. These gestures are ultimately mysterious personal expressions of longing.

The soundtrack in *Day of the Idiots* is probably Schroeter's most improvisational and "noisy"; it is certainly less consistently melodic than in his other films. It is his most anarchic film in terms of sound. Perhaps this is because Schroeter himself did not choose the music, instead it was composed by Peer Raben, who did the music for many of Fassbinder's films. As Carole first enters the asylum there is a barrage of words and sounds that can disorient someone who is viewing the firm for the first time. Someone is screaming; it is Carole's mother pleading with the nurse in the asylum to let her see her child; she screams, "Carole" and "let me see my child." And as Daniel, in *Willow Springs*, ignores his mother when she visits him, so too does Carole ignore her mother's screams. We hear some patients singing the lyrics from a song first heard at the beginning of the film: "a naughty wind one day / raised her skirt right away." And then Mrs. Weber, one of the patients, greets Carole with the words, "Milady, welcome to court." We find out later that she imagines herself as a Russian princess, or Marie Stuart. Then a patient in the foreground, to the far left of the screen, in darkness, utters the words, "stardust from planets / just old slippers in the end…slippers, slippers." There is the sound of bed springs; this is caused by a woman standing on a bed and opening her coat to expose herself to Carole as a much older women next to her says, "you're pretty as a flower, keep your coat closed," and "I'm God and you keep your coat closed." Ula Stöckl who stands near Carole at the entrance slowly moves her outstretched arms while turning in a semi-circle in a kind of trance.

The composite effect of all this improvised poetry and sounds and movements is to render the space highly dramatic. Schroeter writes: "Prague [the film was shot there] itself is a theatrical place, and in line with that, the psychiatric hospital that we built in the studio was an ancient setting outside time — I wanted everything to be surrealistically strange and unreal…." Fragments of poetry echoes in the air for a moment and disappear. We are in a transgressive space, a kind of mad theatre, where players are reciting the words to some mysterious drama. We hear on the soundtrack choir music that almost seems like it's being played at a slower pace than usual. On top of that there is another vocal track. The whole effect is of a kind of sublime chaos made up of high drama with tragic elements. It is also kind of improvised opera. Wolfram Schutte writes: "Once Schroeter has presented this ensemble of 'Women under the influence,' to use the title of a film by John Cassavetes, in a theatre-laboratory fashion, he brings the totally confined characters together polyphonically in the style of an operatic ensemble."

Schroeter also plays with real versus symbolic time in the film. When asked her age, Carole says she is thirteen years old, which would explain her distance from the inmates' activities. It is the same age of Daniel in *Willow Springs*. Thirteen is not her *actual* age, but a kind of symbolic age; I don't know why thirteen was important for Schroeter; could this have been an important age for him since it is when he "came out?" Carole is not so much thirteen years old, but that is how she feels. Finally, just as we are to think he/she with regard to Carole we are not to take the age thirteen as a fact in the real world but in a kind of symbolic space.

The transgressive space opened up in the film also reflects a kind of utopian vision. Schroeter writes:

> I have always felt very close to the psychological inner worlds of the deranged; they are the kind of transgression, lived out in reality, that has always been my subject and a source of inspiration to me. The idea of *Day of the Idiots* was to depict madness in such a way that it connected up with the world outside the hospital.

The shower scenes between the inmates have an "operatic feel" and a "notably queer, fleetingly utopian feeling to them." Several of the women are in the showers, but there is an absence of men. Ellen Umlauf boasts of her sexual prowess in the Eros Center. Magdalena sucks on a woman's finger as she is led about in the bathroom. Ula proudly pisses on another inmate. Magdalena talks of stabbing her husband to death. Ellen leans against the sink, with a seductive expression on her face. The women are playful, erotic, and serious. This is a kind of lesbian utopia. Naked bodies, unafraid, and sexually provocative. Finally, Ula says of Carole as she is leaving the bathroom that she "can't say anything anyway. I think all she can do is fuck." When she hears these words, Carole turns around and her face is seen in close up; she wipes a drop of water from her eye; the expression on her face is sly and suggestive with the vague beginnings of a smile on her lips. With her exit any sense of a utopia comes to an end. This is especially clear when we witness one of the women receiving electroshock and another attempting suicide.

And so the asylum, despite Carole's seeming identification with the patients, briefly pushes her back out into the real world again. She escapes and we see her walking in a kind of bus terminal. An older man approaches, thinking she's a prostitute, and places his hand on her groin; she keeps walking towards the camera; as she does, we hear him say, behind her, "I only touched your cock." We realize that the man thought Carole was a male prostitute; but, as we suggested above, in a sense he was not wrong. She looks like a young boy; and that was clearly intentional on Schroeter's part and something we need to keep in mind as we are watching the film.

Now on the outside, Carole encounters two rows of couples dancing; all together they form two rows and in unison they move their positions and weave among each other; she attempts to walk between the rows of dancers but is defeated and falls down. The rigid formality of the rows of dancers, the formality of marriage, heterosexual coupling, destroys the outsider, the homosexual, the transvestite, who cannot function in the rational world of inherited traditions about what is normal and what is sick. Alexander appears and when she asks him to please help her, he responds nonchalantly, "later." Such indifference crushes her will. In an act of despair, and seeing nowhere else to turn, she readmits herself to the asylum. She is reaching a boiling point of desperation. Throughout the film she had said, "I must not dream," and "I want to breathe," "I want to live." But, as Schroeter writes, "Carole's character in the film does all she can to get sent to the closed asylum, so as to escape from her madness into regulated constraint…" But this constraint proves ultimately too much and ends up blocking her freedom. She is no more able to express her desires here as in the world outside. Carole appears like an outcast in a world of outcasts. Roy Grundmann writes,

> the most intriguing shots are those that position Carole next to open doors, in door frames, and in anterooms or gardens, showing her poised to take advantage of her ability to traverse the institution's boundaries in either direction. But in the context of her resounding failure to find happiness on either side, these shots ultimately mean the opposite of what they, at first glance, seems to signal.

Near the conclusion of the film, she lets out a scream of despair, longing, and of ultimate frustration with the asylum.

Soon after the destruction of the asylum, we see Carole in the street. The view is from the top of a building facing the street.

She walks into traffic, crossing a first street, then a second, being nearly hit by a car, until finally, upon attempting to cross a third street, she is hit by a car and dies. We see her blood-soaked face as she is lying in the street. The scene seems to be a dream. As she is walking, we heard her voice on the soundtrack: "I must not dream," "I must awake," "eyes closed." The scene represents her inability to wake up to reality instead of a kind of fantasy world which the asylum eventually proves to be. As the walls of the asylum fall down at the end of the film, the barrier between patient and normal person is dismantled. We see the patients running into the world, where they will have to confront their fears and the judgement of the world. But importantly, one of the women remains, unable to join the others; even though she is cold and surrounded by the rubble of the collapsed building, she is too afraid and prefers to stay in bed, under the covers. Fear blocks the expression of individuality. Schroeter writes "But most interesting of all are the individual patients: the question of how they stand up to being let out of institutions, and how they overcome their fears." Carole/Schroeter realizes that to go about the world in a dream can prove fatal; one must wake up and face one's fears. About this, Schroeter, has said, "we see the studio set being literally taken apart. But once Carole is outside, dressed as a boy, she can't manage and throws herself in front of a car. It is always up to individuals whether or not they can find freedom for themselves."

During the final credits, we see and hear Ingred Craven, who played a doctor in the film, delivering a monologue on marriage. There are two speakers, A and B, speaking about the married couple, X and Y. A says: "Can you tell me why X married Y of all people." B says: "Because he loves her." A says: "I don't believe that. I guess he chose her because after they'd been together awhile, he felt obligated." B explains X's behavior by attributing it to love and affection. On the other hand, A explains the same behavior by seeing it as an expression of obligatory feelings of guilt. Craven then asks, "How could that possibly happen?" Next, we hear Magdalena say, "Please I want to go back to prison," i.e. the prison of marriage. Craven, herself, was briefly married to the director, Rainer Werner Fassbinder. We could possibly assume that the male, X, is gay. We could assume that the woman, Y, is a lesbian, which could explain the emphasis: "Y *of all people.*" The figure of Swann in Proust's *Swann's Way* is an instance of this phenomenon, since he spent many long hours suffering for a woman whom he realizes at the end of the novel was not even his type. Perhaps Swann's own repressed guilt as a homosexual led to his devoting all his time to a woman who was not "his type." In any event, the monologue is in one sense, concerned with the ways homosexuals get involved with women out of guilt or shame, and it is also a critique of marriage. The only couple in the film, Carole and Alexander, are a disaster. Instead, the inmates are erotic, playful, imaginative, and to an extent free to express themselves. It is a transgressive space and a kind of Utopia that exists outside conventional marriage or a tradition based on the dualities of good and evil, normal and sick. The film concludes, after the screen has gone black, with a statement by Craven: "I want my future."

When Craven says, "I want my future" it is tantamount to saying, "I want to live."

Day of the Idiots is a visually baroque, operatic, highly dramatic film; it is a mysterious examination of identity and of the relation of normative society to its outsiders. Carole is unable to find a place for herself among the inmates nor in her relationship with Alexander. Her intense feeling is unable to find an outlet and thus the only alternative is death. But as we see Carole crossing the streets, we hear her voice detached from the scene, almost describing it to the viewer. Has she dreamed the sequence of her death? Schroeter writes in his memoir about Carole: "In the same year as we made *Day of the Idiots,* she was the James Bond girl in *For Your Eyes Only.* From then on she was a star." Schroeter would survive the demons he exorcised in this film, his bleakest, and go on to make many other films, as well as continuing his work in theatre and directing opera. In 1982, *Day of the Idiots* won the golden award of the German Film Prize.

Works Cited

Grundmann, Roy. "The Passions of Werner Schroeter." In *Werner Schroeter,* ed. Roy Grundmann, 2–56. Vienna: Österreichisches Filmmuseum; Synema-Gesellschaft für Film und Medien, 2018.

Schroeter, Werner, and Claudia Lenssen. *Days of Twilight, Nights of Frenzy.* Translated by Anthea Bell. Chicago: University of Chicago Press, 2017.

Schutte, Wolfram. Booklet included in Werner Schroeter, dir. *Tag der Idioten* (*Day of the Idiots*). Filmmuseum München, 2013, DVD.

Wondratschek, Wolf. Recording of a talk included on Werner Schroeter, dir. *Tag der Idioten* (Day of the Idiots). Filmmuseum München, 2013, DVD.

THE LAST TWO FILMS

Consummation of an Artform

II

A Shadow of Herself:
On Werner Schroeter's *Deux* (2002)

Werner Schroeter's *Deux* (Two) is probably one of his most personal films, composed of memories from childhood and dreams.[1] At the time of its release, Schroeter spoke of the film as his masterpiece, though it has not received much critical attention since then. The skeletal plot revolves around the twins, Marie and Magdelana, both lesbians (both played by Isabelle Huppert), and their mother, Anne, played by Bulle Ogier. It is a film about the nature of the double; Shroeter writes, "the old myths say, truthfully, that those who see themselves in the mirror as a duality, as identity in complete unity, will die." Marie and Magdelana come face to face three times in the film; first, at the opera, where they seem not to fully recognize themselves; later, on a train; and finally, at the incredible climax of the film. Schroeter writes: "Someone sensitive will often follow a train of thought suggesting that he perceives the person who may be a part of himself, but either nothing still links them or too much

---

1   Paul Branco, who produced the film, gave Schroeter great freedom in this film. In his autobiography, Schroeter writes, "In Germany, by contrast, I would have had to keep on explaining why a character did so much as to open or close a door."

does." This is the central complex theme that plays out in the film.

The double or doppelgänger has a rich history in Western thought. There are many stories of alter egos, and double spirits in folklore, myths, and religious concepts. In ancient Egyptian thought, the *ka* was understood as a double with the same feelings and memories of the person to which it is a counterpart. In Finnish mythology, the name for the double is Ankou, a personification of death, and in this manifestation, it appears in Cornish and Breton mythology. In *Deux,* Marie and Magdelena are doubles, but though the films suggests different personalities for each, it becomes difficult, as the film progresses, to tell one from the other. The struggle to unify the two parts is not a struggle between good and evil, but "a split into multiple parts that finds itself in itself, painfully misses its mark, and finally kills itself."

Many characters are introduced into the film to break the structure of 2. There is the twins' mother; the mysterious figure of the serial killer, who places a rose on the victim's body; the twin's lovers; and the young man who commits suicide. As long as the double does not attempt to unify its disparate parts, it is subsumed in the multiple, and the necessary death that the myth requires is forestalled. Duality leads to death, but multiplicity is a goal. Paul B. Preciado, one of the leading thinkers in gender and queer studies, writes, in his book, *An Apartment on Uranus*:

> To talk about sex, gender and sexuality, we have to begin with an act of epistemological rupture, a disavowal of category, a cracking of the conceptual vertebrae to allow for the premises of cognitive emancipation: we must completely abandon the language of sexual difference and sexual identity (even the language of strategic essentialism, as Spivak proposes, or nomadic subjectivity, as Rosi Braidotti proposes). Sex and sexuality now are not the essential property of the subject, but rather the product of various social, discursive technologies, political practices of controlling truth and life

Here, Preciado problematized the dual nature of gender; for Schroeter, the doubling leads to death because of the inability of Marie and Magdelena to unify the split aspects of themselves. When Huppert sees her double at the conclusion of the film, she embraces her, only to kill her. I think this can also be seen, on one level, to resonate with Fassbinder's last film, *Querelle,* and the idea that you kill the one you love. When Huppert's lover professes her love, she seems uninterested, and responds by saying that "it would be ideal if we 'made love' between 10 and 11 pm." Huppert's love for the young man on the bicycle, played by Robinson Stevenin, is ended before it begins by the young man's suicide. Heteronormative desire, maintaining the idea of the double, culminates in death, and romantic love becomes a fiction.

Deux also shows the violence against women in the patriarchy. There are numerous scenes in which men appear aggressive and often mock Huppert. In one scene, that takes place in a café, we see Huppert sitting in a chair, alone, drinking coffee. She is surrounded by men, standing around her in a very stylized manner; one man to her right is wearing a brightly colored red jacket; red is the color of aggression. Soon enough, a man enters Huppert's space, and puts her on his lap; the other's then surround her. There is also the scene where an older man in a car slows down next to Huppert (she is a young girl)[2] and asks her to come home with him. He dresses her in elegant clothing, and wearing a gorgeous dress she dances for him. As she is lying on the bed, she notices him masturbating while watching her. She laughs, but then tears begin to fall. She is sexually inexperienced and watching him, she feels sad. He also teaches her etiquette when eating. If men are not abusive or violent, they idealize a female, and attempt to shape them according to their

2   Huppert is playing a young girl in the film. In his autobiography, Schroeter writes about her age in the film: "It didn't matter to me whether or not one could tell her real age; her stylized appearance was a plus for the story we wanted to tell. In any case a film like *Two* is the total opposite of everyday life, unless one sets out from the true everyday life of the soul that is always there underground, deep down and influential."

143

desires and needs, thus erasing their sense of the themselves as individuals and equal.

The patriarchy is built on a foundation of reason and law, and rejects anything that appears irrational, amateur, unfinished, fragmented, or even lyrical, which shows too much emotion. In another scene, which takes place in a bar or café, Huppert is practicing her singing of opera; we see a man next to her showing disapproval by distorting his facial expressions, until he is clearly mocking her, and growing more and more aggressive. Once again, she is alone, surrounded by aggressive men. Her amateur singing does not seek to command or dominate; she just wants to sing. The men cannot accept that and continue to mock her. Her outpouring of emotion is mocked by the men who then reject her. When she is on the train, shooting heroin, we see a young man watching, and laughing at her, laughing at her despair. Even the transvestite singer of a black vocal group who are singing about the coming of Jesus, assaults her in a nightclub. The male world is aggressive and there is always the threat of violence, particularly when sex is involved. Mckenzie Wark has a similar view of the world which she writes about in his book, *Reverse Cowgirl*. He writes, "Nobody needs to read another story by a man about, well, anything. Certainly not another story where the man fucks the woman. So let's just keep it to this not-novel but less storied dilemma: how does a man whose peak sexual experiences all involved being fucked in the ass go about having sex with a woman." I have always seen the women in Schroeter's films as a projection of his own self in drag. Even in the gay world, it is the femme male who is always at risk of being the victim of violence. Huppert finds resistance even in the gay or trans community. In one scene, as she is walking up the stairs to her apartment, wearing a pink overcoat, wobbling because she is tired or drunk, a woman screams at her, "everybody hates you." Sadly, women turn on their own gender.

Schroeter's film also attacks the family and reproduction because finally, the locus of power is in the nuclear family: "Gender warfare,…is emphasized: while violence is everywhere, the nuclear family is its most important locus and the point from which it radiates outward, de-materializing the virgin, the sinner, the diva. It turns her into a mere shadow of herself." During one scene, while she is travelling on a train, Huppert places a blank sheet of paper on a window, and fervently writes a letter to her parents. In it, she speaks of her "adorable" mother and her "unknown, stern" father. Fatima Naqvi writes, "Family is archive, legacy, transgression, malevolence, subordination, dependency, transmission, and love in all its forms. She stresses the oneiric aspect of the entire film: 'I kiss you, not just as mother, but as the only beings who love me. Not a single day has gone when I didn't dream of you.'" This is the family romance Freud spoke of. Huppert tears up the letter. The scene echoes the opening one in the film, where the twin's mother, Anna, is writing a letter to her daughters, and yet she too tears up her letter. The link is broken, the message unsent.

The scene where the twin's mother is murdered by the serial killer, who may be her husband, played by the same actor, occurs midway through the film, after which she continues to be alive. Effect precedes cause. The distinction between Marie and Magdelena is blurred; they are one person in a timeless myth. Exact scenes are repeated in the film which suggest the cyclical nature of mythical time; but it is this circular pattern that the film wants to disrupt. It is this pattern that reinforces the logical progression of time. Defying this myth allows Huppert to break out of the cage of time, and as if to free-float in an endless stream, where she can bury her alter ego, after consuming her body, and be reborn.

After Huppert murders her double, a figure, who might be the princess of death, tells her that, in order for the dead to arise, she must accept into herself everything about the other. This involves ingesting the rejected, ugly, abject part of herself; here symbolized by the vomit the dead women ejects onto Huppert, and which she has to consume. Schroeter speaks of a detail, in this regard, that he borrowed from the *Thousand and One Nights*; it involved a ghost that appears to a young widow, telling her to eat the first thing she is given, and then she will get her husband back. When the dead man appears, he throws up in her face, she swallows the vomit, and he comes back to life. If I am not ready to accept everything that someone else gives me, I cannot create life: that was the meaning. I brought such ideas from the magical exterior into Two, merging them with the poetry of dark Romanticism.

Tim Fischer, who sings the song that accompanies the scene, speaks of a "blackbird" that he welcomes onto himself, after which he feels that he "understands everything." The dark interior must be incorporated to realize one's identity. The "blackbird" in Tim Fisher's song must be subsumed into himself; it represents knowledge, intuition, spirituality. But for this transformation to occur, as we have seen, the abject, the malformed, the fragmented must be ingested, the body eaten.

Marie/Magdelena transcend death, and in a sense defy the conclusion of the myth of Narcissus. Schroeter writes of the death scene at the conclusion of the film and his borrowing of the Indian myth of the dead:

I also drew inspiration from Indian myths; I made them a part of my personal universe, as a ritual between life and death. There is a custom in India of leading a corpse along on sticks, like a marionette, and literally walking it to its grave. We shot that scene on the beach at night, when Isabelle is burying the alter ego that she has killed and partially eaten, to the ecstatic sound of the tam-tam. And there is a ritual in which the outcast eunuchs of India play music outside houses where children have just been born, telling them the parents that if their child happens to be ugly, they are willing to take it away and raise it. That atavistic way of ensuring that they had progeny was a black symbol in my universe of things.

The film ends with Huppert lying on the beach and speaking the words, "Je t'aime." Then there is a cut. She can finally love herself

A SHADOW OF HERSELF

and the other. The double, becoming multiple, resolves into a unity only in death.[3]

So the double has transitioned from life to death, and escaped like Ariane from the maze of the film. In *Deux,* "one woman's evacuation is no univocal end: Maria/Magdalena…remains on stage." But in fact, throughout the end credits, we see Huppert, radiant, in her elegant dress, her expressions moving from absolute confidence to ecstasy, and ultimately defiance. Released from the labyrinth of the film, she is reborn, transformed, and in death, very much alive on the screen. Huppert as Marie/Magdelena in the film becomes Isabelle Huppert the actress. She lives as her double dies, fully realized as a beautiful person.

Werner Schroeter's *Deux,* is one of his most complex films, largely because it is structured like a dream, and time is not linear but reversible, and even cyclical. But it this cycle of male oppression through dominance and violence, whose locus is the family unit, as well as the prevalence of binary genders, that causes a woman to become almost a shadow of herself. Today, *Deux* is a relevant film because we see increasing nationalism, with its goal of maintaining the heterosexual couple as superior to all others, by invoking God and the importance of the family unit. In this film, Schroeter had his fingers on the future. Thus, he anticipated much of what is now discussed in gender and queer studies, particularly regarding trans men and women. *Deux* was entered in Cannes Film Festival, but the film was unable to find a German distributer. Schroeter tells in his autobiography, of how he was unable to find any interest in the film in Germany, despite his attempts to do all he could. The following is Schroeter's assessment of the film, after viewing it again, a couple of years later:

My private misfortunes cast a dark shadow over my delight in that beautiful total artwork, *Two*. All the same, I was glad that the film was properly screened at the 2002 Cannes Film

---

3 *Deux,* a late film, had the working title of "Ways of Dying." By this time, Schroeter knew he had cancer. The film feels like a kind of final testament.

Festival and was intelligently discussed — except in Germany, where the usual reaction was a total failure to understand it. Incidentally, seeing it again after an interval of some years, I realized that it did not date. For admirers of Isabelle Huppert who also have an eye for Alberte Barsacq'as subtle décor and costumes and Elfi Mikesche's wonderful camerawork, it is an unforgettable experience, but unfortunately, two of the production companies involved found themselves in financial difficulties, and as the situation is not yet clear, *Two* cannot be screened at the moment.

Deux represents the culmination of Schroeter's thinking about film up to this point; it is a complex, subtly political, mythical, fierce and tender, exploration of identity, and gender warfare.

Works Cited

Naqvi, Fatima. "'Psycho' Biography: *Malina* (1991)." In *Werner Schroeter,* ed. Roy Grundmann, 140–57. Vienna: Österreichisches Filmmuseum; Synema-Gesellschaft für Film und Medien, 2018.

Preciado, Paul. *An Apartment on Uranus.* Los Angeles: Semiotext(e), 2019.

Schroeter, Werner, and Claudia Lenssen. *Days of Twilight, Nights of Frenzy.* Translated by Anthea Bell. Chicago: University of Chicago Press, 2017.

Wark, McKenzie. *Reverse Cowgirl.* Los Angeles: Semiotext(e), 2020.

12

A Life Devoted to Art, Music, and Literature: On Werner Schroeter's *Nuit de chien* (2008)

Werner Schroeter's swan song, *Nuit de chien* (This Night), begins with a camera moving over Titian's painting, *The Flaying of Marsyas,* during the opening credit sequence. *The Flaying of Marsyas* was Titian's last painting, completed during a period from 1570–76, in Venice during the plague, that would eventually take his life. The cameraman was not Schroeter but a second-unit cinematographer that he sent to the state museum in Kromeriz, in the Czech Republic to film the painting. In the painting, Apollo slays the satyr, Marsyas, because he fears that he will upstage him in a musical competition between the lyre and the double flute. The central theme of the film is contained in this painting; in essence, the film is about the war between Apollo, the god of reason and law, and Dionysus, the god of the irrational, the poetic, and the natural world, played out in an unknown city sometime in the future. Edward Dimendberg writes:

> Rather than banishing poets from the city, as Plato advocated in *The Republic,* Apollo skins Marsyas alive, a torture

whose sadistic and homosexual overtones are evoked in *The Black Cat* (1934, dir. Edgar G. Ulmer), a film produced in the Universal cycle of horror films, in which Bela Lugosi skins Boris Karlof alive. It also evokes the sado-masochistic eroticism in 1970s photography of Robert Mapplethorpe. Having several years earlier ceased making films in Germany, a country about which by the end of his life he felt ambivalent, Schroeter perhaps imagines himself as Marsyas, a martyr for his art.

Ultimately, in his last film, Schroeter shows his faith in the redemptive quality of art and music, distinct from the brutal aspects of life that offer no sense of redemption.

In the film, the government has fallen, and all the various governmental officials have emptied the state coffers and escaped. What remains in the city are various rebel factions, likely communist; Martins, who is the head of the army, Morasen, the head of the secret police, Barcaralem a kind of independent revolutionary, and a threat to both of them; and then, Gavronsky, one of the most powerful, and intelligent, of them all, and a brilliant strategist. They are all waiting for the arrival, that very night, hence the title of the film, of the mysterious Fraga, who has marshalled his own powerful forces in order to take over the city. Each of these rebel factions are jockeying for power, attempting to gauge the strength of their oppositions, and the possibility of alliances. Morasen is the most brutal, and he attempts to institute his own way of handling men and women in the absence of any laws in the city. Law and order combat the chaotic forces at play in the city.

Ossario arrives by train, into this dark and sinister world. He has come to seek out his lover, Carla Badi, a subversive revolutionary, and to take her away from this dangerous city. But she is nowhere to be found. So, the film begins with an absence, from which the various strands of the plot begin to unfold. Ossario becomes a pawn in a power game whose logic largely escapes him. The man, Manu, was supposed to meet him at a nightclub called the First and the Last and hand over two tickets so that he and Carla could take a boat out of the city, but Manu committed suicide. Martins, the head of the army, wants Ossario to join him. Morasen wants Ossario dead. Martins also wants him to kill Barcarale, and in order to incite Ossario to perform this act, he tells him that Carla was Barcarole's lover, and may be hiding out with him. So the narrative begins to unfold.

Ossario is given bits and pieces of information about Carla. Martins tells him she left the city. Barcarale tells him, after he asks him if he slept with her, that she was a whore. When Gavronsky is asked the same question, he tells Ossario that she was not his type; he also tells her that she was an alcoholic and that he sent her to detox but that she relapsed. This accrual of information contradicts Ossario's image of his wife. As viewers, we can't know for sure the truth or falsity of these statements or the obscure motives that may have led each of these men to make them. What do we really know about each other or about ourselves? Why did Ossario leave his wife in the first place? The evidence in the apartment suggests she either left in a hurry or was kidnapped. Martins on his death bed, after having been shot twice by Morasen, tells Ossario a kind of truth about Clara, but can we trust what he says; why was he elusive at the nightclub; could he have had an affair with her, if we believe what Barcale said about her? Martins finally tells Ossarrio that he should never have left Carla, and that when he left, she fell into a state of despair. He also tells Ossario that he was the only one she loved. This is the most likely of the stories, but is it true? For Schroeter, life itself is ambiguous, and the only truths are those eternal ones we find in "high" art and literature and music.

When Ossario meets the young girl, Vittoria, the film turns away from the ugliness and brutality of the world, and towards a world of sexuality and freedom and beauty. We move from a world that has become unbearable to a space that offers a reprieve, as Art does. In the film, Schroeter displays childhood sexuality in a natural and witty manner. When Ossario, exhausted, lays down in bed, Vittoria asks to lay down beside him;

they are both fully clothed. As Ossario begins to fall asleep, Vittoria nudges her body closer to him, and places her hand on his arm, while her other hand, at her side, fidgets nervously. There is perhaps a desire to use psychology here and invoke Freud on childhood sexuality. But Schroeter has often said that his films are not psychological films and shouldn't be read that way. When Ossario visits his friend, Maria, they have sex in her bathtub. At one point, Vittoria enters the bathroom while they are having sex and asks Ossario to undo the lid on her bottle of orange soda. Shocked and disturbed, he complies with her request. It is a humorous moment in the film. And Maria, teasingly, tells Ossario that he has lost his erection as a result of the episode. Vittoria, on the other hand, seems vaguely curious but restrained with a tinge of surprise mixed with anger or jealousy on her face.

Later, we learn that, while Ossario was visiting Gavronsky, Vittoria attacked Maria in the bathroom of her apartment with scissors. Vittoria is jealous of Maria; of course, a young girl's jealousy is not necessarily the same as an adult's. Vittoria cannot fully articulate her feelings but is acting on impulse when she sees that his attention has been diverted from fully focusing on her. When Vittoria meets a young boy her own age, she asks Ossario if she could take the boy along with them. Ossario says no to her. When Ossario discovered them, as they were showering together, he closed his eyes, not out of shame, but because he seemed to be remembering something perhaps about his own youth; perhaps he is thinking of Carla; the scene is a commentary on the playfulness and instinctive aspect of children, who exist in the here and now because they have no sense of the past or the future, or shame about their bodies. They are innocent of the treachery, and violence that the adults in the film, such as Martins, Mosaren, Barcarole, and Gavronsky, perpetuate. They have no sense of laws or reason; they are governed by their instincts, or primal needs.

In *Nuit de chien,* Schroeter also attacks the Catholic Church for its acts of brutality and evil that has infected the beauty of their churches. Moresan, the chief of the secret police, has his headquarters in a church. From his desk, behind which there is a statue of the crucifixtion above the altar, he orders acts of violence against the men and woman from The First and Last. The image of the crucifixtion is the site for acts of blasphemy and also supplication. Juan, the homosexual waiter at The First and Last, exposes his genitals and buttocks to Jesus on the Cross. He is told by Villar, Masoren's henchman, after asking for protection from the secret police, that they don't protect "faggots" and after attempting to assassinate Morasen, Juan is killed and falls onto the desk, his body having received a multitude of bullets. In another scene, Rosaria folds her hands in prayer, facing a small cross the bare white wall, in the room where she and Irene are being held captive. Irene, after having been beaten almost unconscious, lying in a pool of her own urine on the floor of the church, gazes up at Jesus on the Cross, but is unable to utter a word, as she groans in pain. In his autobiography, Schroeter wrote:

> Figures of the Madonna and Christ suffering on the cross have often drawn attention in my films and theatrical productions, and some people have seen that as either folklore or blasphemy. It has been assumed that the cross that I wear around my neck is a piece of costume jewelry. To say these days that one is a Christian believer often meets with incredulity, but to me, as a convinced Christian, the cross has always meant a great deal. The torturer in *This Night* carries out his interrogations in the cathedral, and his table is not an altar but the desk of a perpetrator of evil deeds. That terrible alliance between the church and power, faith, and brutality was an important statement for me as both a Christian believer and an outspoken critic of the church. The history of the mistakes and crimes of the church is a catastrophe, and the film rejects it as a betrayal.

In the fallen world of the film, the Church allies with the secret police in an attempt to re-establish law and order in a world that is absolutely out of control. Law and order attempts to eradicate the primal forces at work but Art harnesses these same chaotic forces and transforms them into beautiful works.

This complicated plot of *Nuit de chien* reminds me of Howard Hawks's *The Big Sleep.* Upon first viewing that film, one's immediate reaction is perhaps confusion; no answers, no resolution, everything kept vague and indeterminate, like life. We don't get explanations that are immediate and that satisfy the hunger for narrative continuity. Each clue is Janus-faced. Questions accumulate as the momentum of the film builds. And so, we are where Hawks wanted us to be: to feel as Marlowe does, a confused sense of what is happening. Multiple viewings and the perusal of Chandler's novel do solve some of the initial questions. But motive is never clear. Characters tell lies to divert Marlowe's attention. Finally, the film's plot is not so much convoluted as a reflection of the motion of a life lived: the enigma of the real. The way we act in the world most of the time defies explanation and the truth is not absolute. In Schroeter's film, we get the sense that life contains no answers, and that we are led, as if through a labyrinth, in our attempts to make sense of the world. But the journey is more important than the arrival, and truth is only found in art, music, and literature.

To the end of his life (he would die of cancer two years after making the film, in 2010), Schroeter maintained his belief in the power of artistic expression. The film is loaded with literary and musical references. I have already mentioned Titian's painting. Schroeter also used Brahms's Rhapsody in G minor, songs by Federo Garcia Lorca, and "some anonymous Czech music from the nineteenth century"; a Portuguese punk band also appears on stage at The First and Last. In Irene's dream of escape with Rosaria, she says we must escape this "lake of despair,"; the phrase is a reference to the ninth circle of hell in Dante's Inferno, and the large frozen lake, wherein those accused of treachery are placed. And the quote that Schroeter uses at the beginning and at the end of the film is from Act II, Scene 2, of Shakespeare's *Julius Caesar*: "Of all the wonders that I yet have heard, it seems to me the most strange that men should fear; Seeing that death, a necessary end, will come when it will come." Fear of death is what motivates the rebels in the film to commit acts of brutality, and to attempt to dominate and control the people. For Schroeter, "hope resides in acknowledging the inevitability of death and validating the force of beauty"; the beauty of art, music, and literature; the beautiful faces of the children, Vittoria and her desire to feel wanted; her innocence; the unashamed expression of sexual feelings; Ossario and Maria; the dark haired transvestite who appears in several scenes in the film, and who is unafraid when he is teased in a bar, and who escapes the secret police, becomes a figure of strength. Edward Dimendberg writes that Schroeter's "romanticism oscillates between valorizing experiences of transcendence made possible by art, music, sexuality, recognizing their insufficiency, yet nonetheless seeking heightened experiences of life." *Nuit de chien* is one of Schroeter's best films, a powerful summation of a life devoted to music, literature, art, and film.

Works Cited

Dimendberg, Edward. "For and Against Interpretation: *Nuit de chien* (2008)." In *Werner Schroeter,* ed. Roy Grundmann, 178–92. Vienna: Österreichisches Filmmuseum; Synema-Gesellschaft für Film und Medien, 2018.
Schroeter, Werner, and Claudia Lenssen. *Days of Twilight, Nights of Frenzy.* Translated by Anthea Bell. Chicago: University of Chicago Press, 2017.

13

Werner Schroeter and Underground Film

Werner Schroeter lived in New York City during the 1970s and travelled widely throughout the United States so he was familiar with many aspects of American Culture including film, theatre, and literature. In fact, after having seen the American film maker Gregory J. Markopoulos's underground film, *Twice a Man* (1963), at the Knokke-le-Zoute in 1967, he resolved at that moment to be a filmmaker. He also met Candy Darling, the trans actress of Warhol fame, who appeared in *The Death of Maria Malibrun* (1972), in New York, in 1971, when traveling there with his muse, the actress, Magdalena Montezuma. His early films, such as *Neurasia* (1968) and *Argila* (1969) were from a time when he was absorbing and thinking about underground films. I think it would be useful to draw some parallels between what the underground filmmakers surrounding Anthology Film Archives in New York in the '60s and '70s were experiencing in their attempt to avoid the lure of Hollywood and Schroeter's struggles at the beginning of his film career.

So, what is underground film? One quick definition is any film made without commercial considerations. This usually means with little or no budget and a minimum of staff and equipment (perhaps only the filmmaker himself and his camera, and the world in front of him). In his autobiography, Schroeter writes that he began making films as a "dilettante, dealing with everything myself—the camera, the lighting, the cutting, and arranging the music too, because I enjoyed it." Schroeter began making short experimental films, such as his one on the diva, Maria Callas,[1] from slides of her with only the sound of her singing on the soundtrack. Using such a simple set up, the film anticipates much of what would be important in his films: the stylized aspect of the photos, the image of the iconic diva, and the use of opera. They all point to the mannerism that is central to Schroeter's art.

One important and influential film, that reminds me of Schroeter's aesthetic in his early films, is Jack Smith's *Flaming Creatures* (1963). The film uses the same kind of theatrically, over the top drama, and use of popular songs. It is so furious and ecstatic that it defies any absorption into mainstream culture, much like Schroeter's. In *Flaming Creatures,* transvestism is not only a commentary on the gender roles we assume in society but also on the sexual power games in relationships. Transgressing our ideas of submission and domination destabilizes gender roles and, in the film, creates a whirling sexual energy that is ecstatic. The film's metaphysics are so naturally expressed that it's as if Smith would have liked to reconfigure heaven as a place for his "creatures" to roam in an aura of decadent luxury, as if in a nightclub. Space in the film is collapsed, and the viewers are disoriented; the film is, perhaps, calling on us to experience the same dizzying descent into transgressive pleasure. This also reminds me of Schroeter's films, such as *The Death of Maria Malibran.* A fight against the demons of sexuality was waged by many of these filmmakers and constituted a central theme in many underground films, such as those by Carolee Schneemann. I would also include Werner Schroeter among those filmmakers whose films explored sexuality in an unabashed way.

Underground filmmakers in the 60s worked to dismantle the influence of the Hollywood film which stood for popular

---

1   *Maria Callas Portrait* (1968)

entertainment, inflated budgets, hackneyed plots, and behind it all a faceless director orchestrating his puppet show. The auteur theory (which came to prominence in Europe in the mid '50s) did not catch on quickly in the US. And yet the director or film-maker in underground cinema was a kind of auteur operating without the hierarchical structure that Hollywood filmmaking involves; often it was just the filmmaker and his camera, often rented, and perhaps only his friends as "actors." I shot my first few films with a small point and shoot Canon camera, and a few friends and then, in my later films, dispensed with "actors" entirely; I used myself as an "actor" when needed, or random people, and created sixty short films, twenty-four of which were shown at Anthology Film Archives in NYC. Schroeter also used the same actresses in his films, such as Carla Aulaulu, in his early films, and Magdalena Montezuma, who appeared in the early films and many others; she was his muse up until her death; he also occasionally appeared in his early films, such as when he filmed himself directing an actor in *Eika Katappa* (1969).

What unified many of these underground filmmakers was their outsider status: Jonas Mekas was a Lithuanian immigrant, Peter Kubleka, an Austrian, Kenneth Anger was gay, Maya Deren, a voodoo priestess, and Jack Smith was also gay and thought himself the reincarnation of Maria Montez! Schroeter was gay and marginalized. He is the least known of the filmmak-ers of the so-called New German Cinema, though Fassbinder was his good friend and famously supported him. But many of these filmmakers are still not widely known. About Schroeter, William E. Jones writes, "I could recount the injustice of a film culture where Werner Schroeter is invisible, but this would re-quire lending credence to the notion of film culture itself and having faith in institutions to make things right."

In America, these underground filmmakers were brought together in the 60s because they were unified against the sys-tem. System here means the supporters of the Vietnam war, those who opposed Civil Rights, and all those who try to con-strain the freedoms of the mind and the body. These filmmakers had something very real to fight against. What about today? It seems as though artists aspire to join the system rather than fight against it. There is no excuse for that or is there? It boils down to economics. The lure of Hollywood is greater than ever because of the revenue a moderately popular film can generate. But Schroeter had his own ideas about Hollywood:

> I wasn't enthusiastic about Hollywood…There are some American films I admire, like Charles Laughton's *Night of the Hunter,* but that wasn't a classic Hollywood film. And of course there were traces of *Whatever Happened to Baby Jane?* and *Sunset Boulevard* in *Willow Springs.* But my ideas came from Shakespeare, Bellini, Donizetti, and Verdi, not from Hollywood. Despite my travels and adventures in the USA, I consider myself a European artist.

Making it in Hollywood is a risky business, like the stock exchange or the cost of living. Then there is the availability of equipment, university funding, and the Academy of Hollywood which also conscripts ideas from mass or alternative culture for its own purposes. But it will not be entirely comfortable with it acquisitions until it transforms them into something that the masses can consume. I was interested in Schroeter's films because I was also making films without commercial consideration. I could identify with the financial problems Schroeter often spoke about in his autobiography. And mainstream American film culture has largely been unable to assimilate his films in their discourse as evidenced by the paucity of writings about him in English.

Film schools are concerned with techniques and theories. Each graduate leaves prepared with tools to confront the complexities of his time i.e. to earn a living. This reminds me of a funny story. It's said that NYU film students look down upon sexually explicit scenes in films because they are interested in turning a quick profit by exploiting a well-known genre. This is the reason a student film is almost always a horror film or perhaps nowadays, a kind of romantic film. That is, a film that has the potential to make a quick profit before it's converted to DVD and sold on Amazon. But one such filmmaker at NYU entered the porn business quite by chance. His friends laughed at him. But they weren't laughing when he eventually sold his films to *Hustler* magazine for three million dollars! So while film students are reaching for the stars, underground filmmakers have their feet planted firmly on the ground. Most of these students eventually end up teaching in universities. After all, a loft in the East Village costs much more than it did, say, in 1965, because of the Real Estate boom in the '80s, and those wealthy investors who eventually bought up all the properties in Lower Manhattan.

We live in the age of the professional. The word amateur is a derogatory term these days, suggesting someone without the requisite skills or equipment. In this sense, Jack Smith, Kenneth Anger, Harry Smith, Jonas Mekas, Stan Brakhage, Ken Jacobs, Marie Menken, Carolee Schneemann, and Maya Deren are all amateurs. But *inspired* amateurs, nevertheless. People these days attempt to rehabilitate the word amateur by using the contemporary acronym DIY: Do It Yourself. But if you're so inclined, you could also find a copy of *Filmmaking for Dummies* on your kindle! In his biography, Schroeter wrote, "I finally dropped out of my pseudotheoretical studies of film in Munich. I wanted to get at the camera and the cutting table; I wanted to work at my trace in practice and in my mind. Then I did apply to the College of Film in Berlin, and so did Rainer Werner Fassbinder," but they were both rejected. Schroeter continues: "When we spoke at seminars later, the story of that rejection was always good for a laugh."

Remember those 8mm home movies? The small intimate film. What happened to the small intimate film? The personal film? "Don't step on my blue suede shoes" is personal. But also, political. It's about personal freedom. In Schroeter's films the amateur is given center stage. Like these underground filmmakers, Schroeter's films, are intimate, especially when showing the private world of women, without all the special effects of a large production that are common these days. Schroeter's films are also divinely escapist, in that they the world they create is one a viewer can indulge in without the preachiness of so much "intellectual" cinema. Edward Dimendberg writes:

> Whether spectators decide to follow the winding trails of Schroeter's intertexts to their philosophical summits or to forgo interpretation and allow the allusions in the film to wash over them, watching the film is to plunge into erudite melancholy, a grim meditation on mortality whose dense web of citations provides a counterpoint to the violence and terror expounded in the narrative. Intertexuality functions not as a form of bragging intended to burnish the intellectual credentials of Schroeter, but rather proposes the myriad cultural references in the film as viable escape routes — instructions for living — that enable aesthetic transcendence of an intolerable reality.

The films are a catalogue of his obsessions: opera, the diva, silent film, theater, art, literature, and music. It is an intoxicating brew for anyone who wants something original.

These underground filmmakers in America lived through the political and moral outrage of the '60s and created films in opposition to what they saw as an attack on personal freedom, on the self. This movement of filmmakers in New York galvanized around the idea of the inviolability of the self, giving birth to the lyrical film. Rod Grundmann writes, in "The Passions of Werner Schroeter":

> By the mid- to late 70s, after the generation of '68 had undergone a sense of ideological calcification, watching a Schroeter film was considered to be politically revivifying. For Koch, the exalted mimeticism of Schroeter's films brought back memories of cinephile dinner parties during which the guests, inspired by party music, began to gesticulate in the manner of silent film actors, potentially producing a new lexicon of human interaction.

In America, I'm reminded of the diaristic films of Jonas Mekas, and of Stan Brakhage, who emerged from the lyrical film
to become an essayist of the ontological; Kenneth Anger, who
explored the spiritual nature of the self in his own films and
through his exploration of the works of Aleister Crowley; Harry
Smith, who revitalized the art of animation in films that also
contained mystical and occult symbols; he was also, like Anger, a disciple of Aleister Crowley; and Bruce Connor, who le-
gitimized the use of found footage with his politically charged
yet undidactic interpretation of current events. I think of Marie
Menken's wit, and of Joseph Cornell, whose work is entirely created from found footage; or the great humanism and erotic force
of James Broughten's films. But towering above them all, because she was the first to theorize about and make underground
films, is, of course, Maya Deren, whose *Meshes of the Afternoon*
(1945) jumpstarted the movement. Werner Schroeter has carried the torch for free expression in cinematic art, and shares
with many of these filmmakers, particularly Jack Smith, a desire
for excess and theatricality. But it was a freedom that was won
by overcoming obstacles. In his autobiography, Schroeter writes:
"my path was one of organic, autodidactic development. Like
my friends Rainer and Rosa [von Praunheim], I was obliged to
adopt an energetic approach and to overcome obstacles." It is a
great lesson for contemporary filmmakers.

Works Cited

Dimendberg, Edward. "For and Against Interpretation: *Nuit
de chien* (2008)." In *Werner Schroeter,* ed. Roy Grundmann,
178–92. Vienna: Österreichisches Filmmuseum; Synema-
Gesellschaft für Film und Medien, 2018.

Grundmann, Roy, "The Passions of Werner Schroeter." In
Werner Schroeter, ed. Roy Grundmann, 2–56. Vienna:
Österreichisches Filmmuseum; Synema-Gesellschaft für
Film und Medien, 2018.

Schroeter, Werner, and Claudia Lenssen. *Days of Twilight, Nights of Frenzy.* Translated by Anthea Bell. Chicago: University of Chicago Press, 2017.